To Lois! Karen's May
my friend & friend of mine
friend & mine. Life be filled with you
and love.

UPGRADE
YOUR LIFE

UPGRADE YOUR LIFE

21 DAYS
OF PERSONAL TRANSFORMATION

by

DELISHIA A. DAVIS

XULON PRESS

Xulon Press
555 Winderley Pl, Suite 225
Maitland, FL 32751
407.339.4217
www.xulonpress.com

Unless otherwise indicated, Scripture quotations taken from the Holy Bible,
New Living Translation (NLT). Copyright ©1996, 2004, 2015 by Tyndale
House Foundation. Used by permission of Tyndale House Publishers, Inc.

Unless otherwise indicated, Scripture quotations taken from The Message
(MSG). Copyright © 1993, 2002, 2018 by Eugene H. Peterson. Used by
permission of NavPress Publishing Group, represented by Tyndale House
Publishers. Used by permission. All rights reserved.

Paperback ISBN-13: 978-1-66289-913-3
Ebook ISBN-13: 978-1-66289-914-0

Don't copy the behavior and customs of this world, but let God transform you into a new person by changing the way you think. Then you will know what God wants you to do, and you will know how good and pleasing and perfect his will really is (NLT).

Don't become so well-adjusted to your culture that you fit into it without even thinking. Instead, fix your attention on God. You'll be changed from the inside out. Readily recognize what he wants from you, and quickly respond to it. Unlike the culture around you, always dragging you down to its level of immaturity, God brings the best out of you, develops well-formed maturity in you (MSG).

This book is dedicated to my younger daughter, Mycah Alexandrea Davis, who inspires me to strive for excellence each day and overcome every obstacle in my pathway.

Table of Contents

Fasting Information 5
Personal Assessment Pre-Test. 7
The Journey Commitment. 9
Daily Affirmation 11
Daily Prayers. 13
Foreward 17
Preface 19
Introduction 21

Day #1   PATH 25
Day #2   PRAYER 35
Day #3   PARDON. 47
Day #4   PURGE 61
Day #5   PURE HEART 73
Day #6   PRESENCE OF GOD 83
Day #7   PURPOSE 95
Day #8   PREPARATION 105
Day #9   PERSEVERANCE 117
Day #10   PLEASING GOD 129
Day #11   PRAISE 141
Day #12   PURSUIT OF RIGHTEOUSNESS. 151
Day #13   PRIDE 163
Day #14   PROSPERITY. 175
Day #15   PROMISE 187
Day #16   PATIENCE 201

Day #17   PROVISION 213
Day #18   PEACE 231
Day #19   PROCLAMATION 243
Day #20   POSSIBILITIES 253
Day #21   POWER 265

Upgrade Your Life Course Completion Information 278
Personal Transformation Post Test 281
Personal Transformation Success Story 283
Personal Transformation Success Stories 285

Acknowledgments

I am deeply grateful for the love and support of the following individuals and organizations, whose unwavering encouragement has been instrumental in the creation of this book:

To Maya Alexis and Mycah Alexandrea, my beloved daughters, your love and strength inspire me to persevere and prosper.

To Ronald and Helen Boykin, my loving parents, and my sister, Rokisha Reynolds, your unwavering belief in me has been a source of fortitude.

To my wise grandfather, Robert D. Boykin, your guidance and wisdom have shaped my journey in profound ways.

To Gregory and Vanessa Scurlock, Aunt Jessye Lofton, my nieces and my dear goddaughters – Angel, Antoniette, Ariana, Asia, Brianna, Brittnye, DeLishia, LaKatherine and Lolina – your presence in my life fills it with joy and purpose.

To my adopted sons – Titus, Diron, Nickayl, Jeremiah, Justin, David, Aaron, and Alvis – your resilience and love uplift me daily.

To Calloway United Methodist Church, the Arlington Coalition of Black Clergy, the National Council of Negro Women, the National Association for the Advancement of Colored People, People for the American Way, Clergywomen's Prayer Group, and the African American Ministers Leadership Council, thank you for your unwavering support and commitment to justice and equality.

To my friends Ronda, Andrea, Ayanna, Donnessa, Elaine, Gertrude, Martin, Mary, Tracey, Peter, and others who remain near and dear–your friendship and camaraderie bring light into my life.

To Bishops Messiah, McKenzie, and Otoo, Mother Messiah, Pastor Yankson, my prayer partners, Sorors, ministry colleagues, clients, former congregants, and ministry partners, your collaboration and shared passion have enriched my journey beyond measure.

And finally, to all those who love me and whom I love, your unwavering support and encouragement sustain me through every challenge. Thank you for being my pillars of strength and inspiration.

In Loving Memory

I acknowledge the cherished memories of those who have touched my life deeply and left an indelible mark on my heart:

Earl W. Brent	Dudley Darnell Proctor
Henry and Florence Ross	Marvin Wentz Turner
Helena Hall Boykin	Flora L. Henderson
Kenneth Ross	Alice Tobias Miller
Pauline Griffin	James H. Lofton
Carrie Hardy	Lordian Peter Turner
Bonita Faye Jones	Rev. Diane Ross Brown
Lewis and Linda Tatem	Etelka Robinson Griffin
David L. Brown	Norman Lear
Tony D'Angelo Foy	George E. Hazzard
Raelicia Andrea Glenn	Dr. Joseph Lowery
Bishop Steven J. Smith	Dr. Cain Hope Felder

May their legacies live on in the hearts and minds of those who knew and loved them. Though they may be gone from our sight, they will forever remain alive in our memories.

Sample Personal Transformation Schedule

Morning Devotion (30 minutes):

Begin with a Daily Affirmation to set the tone for the day.

Engage in Prayer, expressing gratitude and seeking guidance.

Read Scriptures and reflect on their meaning, focusing on the memory verse for the day. Complete Personal Assessment Exercises, examining areas of personal growth and reflection.

Evening Reflection (20 minutes):

Set aside time for quiet Reflection and Revelation, reviewing the events of the day and seeking insights.

Work on Personal Growth Assignment, focusing on areas of improvement and goal setting.

Journal for the day, documenting thoughts, feelings, and experiences.

Prayer Focus (10 minutes):
Throughout the Day, dedicate 10 minutes to Special Prayer directed by the Prayer Focus for the day, focusing on specific intentions or concerns.

This structured schedule allows for dedicated time each day to nurture spiritual growth, reflection, and connection with the divine, fostering a deeper sense of inner peace and purpose. Please create the schedule that works best for your spiritual growth and development.

ESSENTIALS FOR THIS PERSONAL TRANSFORMATION

- A notebook or prayer journal

- A quiet place to pray and study

- An accountability partner

- Access to internet to access supplemental resources

- An open heart for transformation

- A relationship with Almighty God

- Perseverance to continue the journey for the entire time

Fasting Information

Fasting is a personal choice to deepen your relationship with God. You choose the type of fasting experience and your level of commitment to the journey. Below are suggestions for you to consider in making the final decision as you begin the time of upgrade in your life.

Embarking on a Daniel Fast involves a 21-day period of prayer and fasting, inspired by the biblical story of Daniel. This spiritual journey typically includes a plant-based diet, avoiding certain foods, and focusing on prayer and reflection. It's seen as a way to draw closer to God, seeking guidance and spiritual growth. During the fast, participants often abstain from meat, sweets, and processed foods, instead opting for fruits, vegetables, and whole grains. This dietary shift is combined with intentional prayer and meditation. Reading relevant scriptures, journaling, and attending group gatherings can enhance the experience.

For those seeking alternative fasting options, abstaining from television, shopping, or personal pleasures can also be impactful. Disconnecting from media, materialism, or distractions allows for greater focus on spiritual development and self-awareness. Remember, the key lies in sincere intention, self-discipline, and a commitment to spiritual enrichment.

Please prayerfully consider your method of fasting and make the commitment as you prepare for the 21-day journey of personal transformation.

Personal Assessment

Rate yourself by the following statement on a scale of 1 to 10. 1 = poor, 10 = excellent

I kept my word on every promise last year. 1 2 3 4 5 6 7 8 9 10

My family can trust me. 1 2 3 4 5 6 7 8 9 10

I gave my all to accomplishing goals in the last six months. 1 2 3 4 5 6 7 8 9 10

I read my Bible every day last month. 1 2 3 4 5 6 7 8 9 10

When I encounter a personal trial, I talk to God first. 1 2 3 4 5 6 7 8 9 10

I never doubt God. 1 2 3 4 5 6 7 8 9 10

God can trust me. 1 2 3 4 5 6 7 8 9 10

I am a tither. 1 2 3 4 5 6 7 8 9 10

I do not overindulge in anything. 1 2 3 4 5 6 7 8 9 10

I help those in need. 1 2 3 4 5 6 7 8 9 10

I sacrifice for others. 1 2 3 4 5 6 7 8 9 10

I am unselfish. 1 2 3 4 5 6 7 8 9 10

I am humble. 1 2 3 4 5 6 7 8 9 10

I care about how I make other people feel. 1 2 3 4 5 6 7 8 9 10

I am not addicted to anything. 1 2 3 4 5 6 7 8 9 10

I read books and articles to stimulate my intellect weekly.
1 2 3 4 5 6 7 8 9 10

I study God's word. 1 2 3 4 5 6 7 8 9 10

I attend public worship on a regular basis. 1 2 3 4 5 6 7 8 9 10

I do not complain when people ask me to do something.
1 2 3 4 5 6 7 8 9 10

I pray daily. 1 2 3 4 5 6 7 8 9 10

I do not lie or omit the truth. 1 2 3 4 5 6 7 8 9 10

I love my enemies. 1 2 3 4 5 6 7 8 9 10

I have not abandoned my family or loved ones in a time of need.
1 2 3 4 5 6 7 8 9 10

I have asked for forgiveness every time I hurt someone in any way.
1 2 3 4 5 6 7 8 9 10

I am in right relationship with God. 1 2 3 4 5 6 7 8 9 10

I do not hate anyone. 1 2 3 4 5 6 7 8 9 10

I am faithful to every commitment I made. 1 2 3 4 5 6 7 8 9 10

I have never used or abused anyone. 1 2 3 4 5 6 7 8 9 10

I do not harbor any anger or resentment. 1 2 3 4 5 6 7 8 9 10

I am ready to move forward in my life. 1 2 3 4 5 6 7 8 9 10

Personal Transformation Commitment

———◦❖❖❖◦———

_____

Today's Date

Dear God,

I want to experience spiritual renewal in my life. I understand that requires a commitment from me. I hereby commit to daily devotions each day at _____ am/pm. Also, I will fast from _____ _____ for the entire twenty-one days of this journey. I want to grow through this experience, so I choose _____ as my accountability partner. I will contact my accountability partner each day of the journey and share at least one thing I have gained during this experience. I thank you in advance for answering my prayer about _____ _____ and I avail myself to your will concerning my life.

Sincerely,

_____

Signature

Daily Affirmation

I am a child of God. I was chosen by God to walk in prosperity and experience divine power. Today, I will experience miracles, signs and wonders as I put my faith in God. I cancel any evil assignments directed at my faith, finances or family. I declare supernatural power and generational blessings over every part of my life. The work I perform today will bless many generations to come. I am victorious and I will overcome any obstacle in my path. God will exceed my expectations today, and I will give God all the glory for every blessing, triumph and victory. In my life, the best is yet to come. Amen.

Morning Prayer

Dear God,

As I embark on this journey of personal transformation, I come before you seeking your guidance, strength, and grace. I ask for your presence to be with me every step of the way, illuminating the path of growth and renewal that lies ahead.

Grant me the peace that surpasses all understanding, Lord. Calm my anxious thoughts and fill my heart with tranquility as I navigate the challenges and changes that come with transformation. Let your peace reign in my mind and spirit, anchoring me in your unwavering love.

I also ask for joy to accompany me on this journey. Help me to find moments of delight and gratitude amidst the trials and tribulations. May my heart be filled with the joy that comes from knowing you and experiencing your transformative power in my life.

God, I seek your direction as I strive for personal transformation. Guide my steps, illuminate my mind, and open my heart to the changes you desire to bring about within me. Lead me to the places, people, and experiences that will shape me into the individual you have called me to be.

Furthermore, I lift up my mind and body to you, asking for your healing touch. Heal any wounds that hinder my growth, whether they be physical, emotional, or spiritual. Grant me the strength to over-come obstacles and the resilience to face challenges with grace and perseverance.

In the name of Jesus, I pray for a renewed mind and a healthy body, so that I may fully embrace the journey of personal transformation that lies before us. Amen.

Evening Prayer

Dear God,

As the night falls and the world around me quiets down, I come to you with an open heart and a humble spirit. I surrender my life to you, knowing that you are the ultimate source of peace and direction.

I ask for your guidance in all aspects of my life. Show me the path you have planned for me and give me the strength to follow it. Help me to trust in your timing and to have faith in your plan for my life.

Lord, I pray for peace in my heart and mind. Calm the anxieties and worries that keep me up at night. Fill me with your presence and grant me the peace that surpasses all understanding.

I trust in your wisdom and love, knowing that you have the best intentions for me. Thank you for being my rock and my refuge, especially in the darkness of the night.

In Jesus' name, I pray. Amen.

Foreward

This book is a powerful tool that will guide you on a journey of self-discovery and personal growth. Through daily reflections, exercises, and practical tips, you will embark on a transformative 21-day experience that will enhance your life in immeasurable ways.

I can personally attest to the impact of this book, as it has made a significant difference in my own life. The daily readings and exercises have helped me to become a better version of myself, both personally and spiritually. As a Christian, I have found that this book has deepened my faith and helped me to live a more fulfilling and purposeful life.

I encourage you to open your heart and mind to the wisdom and guidance within these pages. Embrace the journey of personal transformation and allow this book to empower you to make positive changes in your life. I am confident that you will find this book to be an excellent resource that will help you to grow and thrive in all areas of your life.

Get ready to embark on a 21-day journey that will leave a lasting impact on your life. I am excited for you to experience the transformation that awaits you.

Rev. Dr. Joseph Lowery
Atlanta, Georgia
(1921-2020)

Preface

I am elated that you will Upgrade Your Life through the 21 Days of Personal Transformation! This will be a powerful, life changing season for you. You have experienced many things in life, and one thing is for sure – it's time to take it to the next level. This journey is not intended for those who are satisfied with everything in their lives and do not want change; this journey is for people who have actively chosen to become wiser, stronger and better in this new season!

This prayer journey is not as simple as reading a book; it will require reflective thought, dedication, accountability and determination to complete this journey. You will realize your visions, dreams and goals!

The Prayer Journey has three parts, and you are encouraged to participate in all parts or the ones you are prepared for at this stage of your life. For maximum growth, I highly recommend all three parts of the journey simultaneously. The three parts are:

~ **Personal devotion**: Positive affirmations, morning and evening prayers are included to guide your devotional time each morning. Additionally, there are Bible verses to read and personal assessments with a specific topic based upon the daily focus. This time of study will require approximately 15 minutes each morning before you begin any personal duties or responsibilities. Also, there is a journal page to write your thoughts and feelings each day. This will enable you to look back at this time and measure your personal transformation and spiritual growth.

~ **Fasting:** Fasting simply means to refrain from something in life as a sacrifice. Participants are encouraged to sacrifice during this time; however, your personal fast is between you and the Lord. You can choose to fast from television, internet, soft drinks, football season, food, etc. Please pray and decide how you will fast and remain consistent for the entire 21 days.

~ **Accountability:** We all need an Accountability Partner during the time of Personal transformation. Please choose wisely – find someone that will encourage and inspire you along the way.

Prepare yourself now! It will not always be easy, but the benefits are out of this world. I am looking forward to sharing with you on this journey and realizing our goals and dreams. You will fulfill God's purpose for your life! I declare for you — the best is yet to come.

Pastor DeLishia A. Davis

Introduction

Today, I invite you on a transformative journey towards a better life. Each of us carries the potential for growth and change within us, but it requires courage and commitment to step into the fullness of who we are meant to be. In Romans 12:2, we are urged, "Do not conform to the pattern of this world, but be transformed by the renewing of your mind." This transformation begins with a willingness to embrace new possibilities and to take intentional steps towards positive change.

> Each of us carries the potential for growth and change within us, but it requires courage and commitment to step into the fullness of who we are meant to be.

For the next 21 days, I invite you to join in this journey of transformation, which is an upgrade for your life. You will embark on a path of self-discovery, growth, and renewal. Each day, the journey will guide you in an exploration of different aspects of your life – thoughts, habits, relationships, and goals – and provide guidance and direction in taking the practical steps towards upgrading and enhancing every detail of your life.

This journey is not about perfection, but making intentional progress in your life. It's about embracing the journey of becoming the best version of yourself, one day at a time. As recorded in Philippians 3:13-14, "Brothers and sisters, I do not consider myself yet to have taken hold of it. But one thing I do: Forgetting what is behind and straining toward what is ahead, I press on toward the goal to win the prize for which God has called me heavenward in Christ Jesus."

Throughout these 21 days, you will receive specific guidance and information to deepen your faith and establish plans for the future.

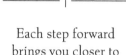

Each step forward brings you closer to the life of abundance and purpose that God desires for you.

Personal transformation is guaranteed through the power of prayer, seeking God's guidance and exercising perseverance through the challenges and opportunities that come your way. It is important to celebrate every small victory, knowing that each step forward brings you closer to the life of abundance and purpose that God desires for you.

You can access the Upgrade My Life course online and join the supportive community of prayer partners and others seeking personal transformation. There are also messages of empowerment, affirmation and motivation for you each day. Your life will be enriched in immeasurable ways as you do the internal work, which will result in external blessings and benefits.

I invite you to take the first step towards a better life today. Join in this journey of transformation and upgrade your life for the glory of God and the fulfillment of your highest potential. Are you ready to take the challenge? Let's begin this journey together, with faith and expectancy in our hearts. Amen.

"God often leads us on journeys we would never take if it were up to us. Don't be afraid. Take courage. Have faith. Trust God."

Eugene Cho

Day One

Word for the day: **PATH**

Welcome to the first day on your journey towards excellence and greatness! Today, we will evaluate your current path and what is in control of your life. As Christians, we must make sure that Jesus is not only our Savior, but our Lord. To call him Savior means he kept you from destruction, but reverencing him as Lord means he is in control. Often times, we make decisions and ask the Lord to bless them, but the proper way is to ask the Lord what path we should take in the first place. Today, make a promise to cancel your plans and follow the path the Lord has in store for you. This decision will lead you to a place of promise.

Blessings!

Pastor D

BIBLICAL PASSAGES

Psalm 27

"The LORD is my light and my salvation — so why should I be afraid?
The LORD protects me from danger — so why should I tremble?
When evil people come to destroy me, when my enemies and foes attack
me, they will stumble and fall.
Though a mighty army surrounds me, my heart will know no fear. Even
if they attack me, I remain confident.
The one thing I ask of the LORD — the thing I seek most — is to live in
the house of the LORD all the days of my life, delighting in the LORD's
perfections and meditating in his Temple.

For he will conceal me there when troubles come; he will hide me in
his sanctuary. He will place me out of reach on a high rock.
Then I will hold my head high, above my enemies who surround me.
At his Tabernacle I will offer sacrifices with shouts of joy, singing and
praising the LORD with music.
Listen to my pleading, O LORD. Be merciful and answer me!
My heart has heard you say, 'Come and talk with me.' And my heart
responds, 'LORD, I am coming.' Do not hide yourself from me. Do not
reject your servant in anger. You have always been my helper. Don't
leave me now; don't abandon me, O God of my salvation!
Even if my father and mother abandon me, the LORD will hold me close.
Teach me how to live, O LORD. Lead me along the path of honesty, for
my enemies are waiting for me to fall.
Do not let me fall into their hands. For they accuse me of things I've
never done and breathe out violence against me.
Yet I am confident that I will see the LORD's goodness while I am
here in the land of the living.
Wait patiently for the LORD. Be brave and courageous. Yes, wait
patiently for the LORD."

Psalm 25

"To you, O LORD, I lift up my soul. I trust in you, my God! Do not let me be disgraced, or let my enemies rejoice in my defeat. No one who trusts in you will ever be disgraced, but disgrace comes to those who try to deceive others. Show me the path where I should walk, O LORD; point out the right road for me to follow. Lead me by your truth and teach me, for you are the God who saves me. All day long I put my hope in you. Remember, O LORD, your unfailing love and compassion, which you have shown from long ages past. Forgive the rebellious sins of my youth; look instead through the eyes of your unfailing love, for you are merciful, O LORD.

The LORD is good and does what is right; he shows the proper path to those who go astray.

He leads the humble in what is right, teaching them his way. The LORD leads with unfailing love and faithfulness all those who keep his covenant and obey his decrees. For the honor of your name, O LORD, forgive my many, many sins.

Who are those who fear the LORD? He will show them the path they should choose. They will live in prosperity, and their children will inherit the Promised Land. Friendship with the LORD is reserved for those who fear him. With them he shares the secrets of his covenant. My eyes are always looking to the LORD for help, for he alone can rescue me from the traps of my enemies. Turn to me and have mercy on me, for I am alone and in deep distress. My problems go from bad to worse. Oh, save me from them all! Feel my pain and see my trouble. Forgive all my sins. See how many enemies I have, and how viciously they hate me! Protect me! Rescue my life from them! Do not let me be disgraced, for I trust in you. May integrity and honesty protect me, for I put my hope in you. O God, ransom Israel from all its troubles."

PERSONAL ASSESSMENT

Please answer the following questions with detail.

1. Are you pleased with the current path you are on in life?

   _____

   _____

2. What things or situations have caused you to get off the path?

   _____

   _____

3. Are any people in your life distractions from the path?

   _____

   _____

4. Who has made the major decisions in your life?

   _____

   _____

5. How were decisions regarding your life made in the past year?

   _____

   _____

6. What have been the hardest things for you to face in life?

   _____

   _____

7. Do you have a plan for your life and future?

   _____

   _____

LIFE TRANSFORMATION MESSAGE

In a world filled with uncertainty and challenges, it can be easy to rely on our own understanding and plans. However, the Bible reminds us of the wisdom and guidance that comes from entrusting our lives to God.

In Proverbs 3:5-6, we are encouraged to trust in the Lord with all our hearts and lean not on our own understanding. We are reminded to acknowledge God in all our ways, and God will direct our paths. This verse serves as a powerful reminder that God's wisdom far surpasses our own, and when we surrender our plans to Him, He will lead us in the right direction.

Similarly, in Psalm 32:8, the Lord promises, "I will instruct you and teach you in the way you should go; I will counsel you with my loving eye on you." This verse reassures us that God longs to guide us and teach us the best way to live. When we allow God to direct our paths, we can rest assured that God will lead us with love and compassion.

Letting God direct our paths requires us to be open to God's leading, to seek God's will through prayer and to meditate on God's Word. It means surrendering our desires and plans to God's perfect and sovereign will, trusting that God knows what is best for us.

As we navigate the complexities of life, let us remember the words of Proverbs 16:9, "In their hearts humans plan their course, but the Lord establishes their steps." This verse reminds us that while we may make plans, it is ultimately God who determines our steps and guides us along the way.

So, let us have faith in God's guidance, trust in God's wisdom, and surrender our paths to God. When we allow God to direct our lives, we can rest in the assurance that God will lead us on a path of purpose, fulfillment, and abundant life.

> When we allow God to direct our lives, we can rest in the assurance that God will lead us on a path of purpose, fulfillment, and abundant life.

The path we take in life is important in determining our destiny and timetable. In the Old Testament, the children of Israel were on a journey that should have taken days but took many years because of their choices, disobedience and distractions.

Likewise, you and I have had visions, dreams and goals for years, but it seems that there is always something to get in the pathway. However, as Bishop T.D. Jakes says, *"A Delay is not a Denial."*

Similar to the children of Israel, we have wasted precious time, energy and resources along this pathway. We should be much further in the path, but turns and detours have lengthened the process. Today, we must say ENOUGH. It is your time and season for a powerful breakthrough and to receive exponential blessings in your life.

Like the Lord Jesus said in the garden of Gethsemane, today we must pray, "Not my will, but thy will be done." Surrender this new day, month, season and year to the Lord and follow the prescribed path for the future. The best is yet to come!

May we all seek God's direction and trust in God's plans for our lives. Amen.

PERSONAL TRANSFORMATION ASSIGNMENT

1. Pray specifically in the morning about the vision and path for your life.

   _____

   _____

2. Read the following scriptures and write them in your own words: Proverbs 4:26; Psalm 1:6; Proverbs 2:20

   _____

   _____

3. Write the vision and goal plan the Lord has given you for this year. Map out a phase to accomplish each month.

   _____

   _____

4. What do you hope to accomplish in the next five years?

   _____

   _____

5. What do you hope to accomplish in the next ten years?

   _____

   _____

PRAYER
Lord, I release my will and I seek your will for my life, in the name of Jesus. Amen

JOURNAL ENTRY

(Please use this space or your own book designated for this time.)

Lord, I submit my will regarding

_____

_____

_____

_____

I surrender

_____

_____

_____

_____

I request

_____

_____

_____

_____

Please lead me

_____

_____

_____

_____

"Lord, make me an instrument of thy peace.
Where there is hatred, let me sow love,
Where there is injury, pardon;
Where there is doubt, faith;
Where there is despair, hope;
Where there is darkness, light;
And where there is sadness, joy.

O Divine Master, grant that I may not so much seek
to be consoled as to console,
to be understood as to understand,
to be loved, as to love.

For it is in giving that we receive,
It is in pardoning that we are pardoned,
and it is in dying that we are born to eternal life."

— **St. Francis of Assisi**

"Prayer is a form of communication between God and man and man and God... I am always impressed by the fact that it is recorded that the only thing that the disciples asked Jesus to teach them how to do was to pray."

~ Howard Thurman
Disciplines of the Spirit, 1977

Day Two

Word for the day: **PRAYER**

It's Day #2 of our journey! By now, you have committed to devotional time, a personal fast and accountability. It is wonderful to speak with others, but there is nothing like communication with God! Today, we will focus our attention on prayer. We must pray daily to make it through this journey and ultimately to be transformed personally.

Communication is the key to a successful relationship. It is an opportunity to nurture your relationship. No one wants to be in a one-sided relationship where the other person does not listen to them or make the development of the relationship a priority.

In our relationship with Almighty God, prayer is our method of communication. During this consecrated time and throughout your life, you can speak to God and God speaks back to you. Prayer is critically important to a Christian's walk with God.

Throughout the Bible, there are references to summon the people of God to prayer, especially in moments of crisis and peculiar joy. This journey is your personal summons. Make it a priority to begin your day with prayer and seek the will of God in all things.

As you pray, remember to speak as well as listen. A method of prayer that I follow often is ACTS – Adoration, Confession, Thanksgiving and Supplication. Begin with praise and **adoration** of Almighty God for who God is in your life, then **Confess** your sins and shortcomings. Afterward, take time to express **Thanksgiving** for the many blessings and lastly, in **supplication**, ask for the things you need and desire in life.

Regardless of your method, the Lord will reward you when you sincerely and earnestly seek God's will. Do not allow anything or anyone to keep you from the place God is calling you to! Keep your heart and mind focused on the will of God and nurture your spirit by communicating with God.

In all seasons of your life, take time to pray and seek the will of the Lord. The benefits are out of this world!

Greater is coming!

Pastor D

BIBLICAL PASSAGES

"Seek the Lord and his strength, seek his presence continually" (1 Chronicles 16:11 NRSV).

"Rejoice in the Lord always. I will say it again: Rejoice! Let your gentleness be evident to all. The Lord is near. Do not be anxious about anything, but in everything, by prayer and petition, with thanksgiving, present your requests to God. And the peace of God, which transcends all understanding, will guard your hearts and your minds in Christ Jesus. Finally, brothers, whatever is true, whatever is noble, whatever is right, whatever is pure, whatever is lovely, whatever is admirable—if anything is excellent or praiseworthy—think about such things" (Philippians 4:4-8).

"And when you pray, do not be like the hypocrites, for they love to pray standing in the synagogues and on the street corners to be seen by men. I tell you the truth, they have received their reward in full. But when you pray, go into your room, close the door and pray to your Father, who is unseen. Then your Father, who sees what is done in secret, will reward you. And when you pray, do not keep on babbling like pagans, for they think they will be heard because of their many words. Do not be like them, for your Father knows what you need before you ask him. This, then, is how you should pray: 'Our Father in heaven, hallowed be your name, your kingdom come, your will be done on earth as it is in heaven. Give us today our daily bread. Forgive us our debts, as we also have forgiven our debtors. And lead us not into temptation, but deliver us from the evil one.' For if you forgive men when they sin against you, your heavenly Father will also forgive you. But if you do not forgive men their sins, your Father will not forgive your sins.

"When you fast, do not look somber as the hypocrites do, for they disfigure their faces to show men they are fasting. I tell you the truth, they have received their reward in full. But when you fast, put oil on your head and wash your face, so that it will not be obvious to men that you are fasting, but only to your Father, who is unseen; and your Father, who sees what is done in secret, will reward you" (Matthew 6:5-18).

"Be joyful always; pray continually; give thanks in all circumstances, for this is God's will for you in Christ Jesus" (1 Thessalonians 5:16-18).

PERSONAL ASSESSMENT

Please answer the following questions with detail

1. How often do you pray?

    _____

    _____

2. Do you pray for yourself?

    _____

    _____

3. Do you intercede for others?

    _____

    _____

4. How do you respond to overwhelming, stressful situations?

    _____

    _____

5. Do you incorporate scripture0 into your prayers?

    _____

    _____

6. How can you improve your prayer life?

    _____

    _____

LIFE TRANSFORMATION MESSAGE

Today, we commit to explore a fundamental aspect of our faith—prayer. Prayer is not merely a ritual or a set of words we recite; it is the lifeline of our relationship with God. Just as communication is crucial in any human relationship, prayer is essential in our walk with the Lord.

————†————

Prayer is essential in our walk with the Lord.

It is through prayer that we connect with the Divine, express our deepest longings, and align our will with His. Let us delve into the importance of prayer and how it strengthens our bond with God.

Imagine a relationship without communication. It would be distant, misunderstood, and ultimately, it would wither. Similarly, our relationship with God thrives on communication. Prayer is the means by which we converse with our Creator. Through prayer, we express our adoration, confess our sins, give thanks, and present our requests. Philippians 4:6-7 reminds us, "Do not be anxious about anything, but in everything by prayer and supplication with thanksgiving let your requests be made known to God. And the peace of God, which surpasses all understanding, will guard your hearts and your minds in Christ Jesus."

In the Garden of Gethsemane, Jesus prayed, "Not my will, but Yours be done" (Luke 22:42). Prayer is not about convincing God to do our bidding but about transforming our hearts to desire His will. When we pray, we open ourselves to the guidance of the Holy Spirit, seeking God's wisdom and surrendering our plans to divine purpose. This alignment brings us peace, knowing that our lives are in the hands of a loving and sovereign God.

Life is filled with challenges, trials, and uncertainties. In these moments, prayer becomes our refuge. Psalm 46:1 says, "God is our refuge and strength, a very present help in trouble." Through prayer, we find solace and strength, knowing that God is with us, listening to our cries and comforting us in our distress. The act of praying itself can bring calm to our hearts, reminding us that we are not alone in our struggles.

Just as our bodies need nourishment, our spirits need prayer to grow. Prayer deepens our relationship with God, fostering a greater understanding of divine character and unconditional love for us. When we spend time in prayer, we become more attuned to God's voice, more sensitive to divine leading, and more reflective of covenantal love. It is through this ongoing dialogue that our faith is strengthened and our spiritual lives enriched.

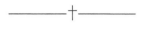

> When we spend time in prayer, we become more attuned to God's voice, more sensitive to divine leading, and more reflective of covenantal love.

Intercessory prayer—praying on behalf of others—is a powerful expression of love and faith. James 5:16 tells us, "The prayer of a righteous person is powerful and effective." When we pray for others, we participate in God's work in their lives, standing in the gap and lifting them up to the Father. This act of selflessness not only blesses those we pray for but also cultivates a heart of compassion within us.

> Prayer is not just a duty; it is a profound privilege.

In conclusion, prayer is not just a duty; it is a profound privilege. It is the heartbeat of our relationship with God, the channel through which we communicate, align our will with His, find strength and comfort, grow spiritually, and intercede for others. Let us commit ourselves to a life of prayer, embracing the promise that when we draw near to God, He will draw near to us (James 4:8). As we pray, may our relationship with our Creator grow deeper, richer, and more intimate, transforming our lives and the world around us.

PERSONAL TRANSFORMATION ASSIGNMENT

1. Read the following scriptures and write at least three of them in your own words: Psalm 4:1, Proverbs 15:29, Romans 8:26, Colossians 4:2, 1 Thessalonians 5:17, James 1:5-7, James 5:16.

   _____

   _____

2. What does Proverbs 15:29 mean at this stage of your life?

   _____

   _____

3. Name a biblical character that had a strong prayer life. Give three characteristics about that person.

   _____

   _____

4. How would you explain 1 Thessalonians 5:17 to a new believer?

   _____

   _____

5. Name a person in your life (past or present) that is a true prayer warrior.

   _____

   _____

6. How did that person influence your life?

   _____

   _____

7. Jamesina is a college student who grew up in a Muslim household. She has recently accepted the Lord as her personal Savior but does not know how to pray. Write three things you could tell her in this situation.

_____

_____

8. Mother Harris is an 84-year-old church mother who learned to pray by reciting church language and does not speak from her heart. She recently confessed that she has never heard from God. What could you suggest to Mother Harris as ways to improve her prayer life?

_____

_____

9. How are you like Jamesina or Mother Harris? Be specific

_____

_____

10. What advice will you apply to your own prayer life?

_____

_____

11. What commitments will you make today for a more intimate prayer life?

_____

_____

12. Write a prayer that you will pray each day during the journey. Keep it in your personal devotional space for daily reflections.

_____

_____

PRAYER

Prayer: Holy God, we thank You for the gift of prayer, the precious privilege of communicating with You. Help us to be faithful in our prayer lives, seeking Your face daily and aligning our hearts with Yours. Strengthen us through prayer, comfort us in our trials, and guide us in Your truth. May our prayers reflect our love for You and our desire to know You more. In Jesus' name, I pray. Amen.

JOURNAL ENTRY

(Please use this space or your own book designated for this time.)

My prayer life is

_____

_____

_____

_____

In my prayer life, I want to change the following:

_____

_____

_____

_____

Lord, please help me

_____

_____

_____

_____

Please bless

_____

_____

_____

_____

"There is no sin that God can not pardon.
All we need is ask for forgiveness."

—Pope Francis

Day Three

Word for the day: **PARDON**

It's day #3 of the journey already! After spending time in communication with the Lord, it is very clear that we need divine forgiveness for our errors and sins. Over time, we have fallen short of the expectations of a child of God. However, we serve a loving and forgiving God. Today, pause to seek divine forgiveness and to be cleansed by God. Also, you will release others who have wronged you. Today, you will move forward as you experience the forgiveness and love of the Lord.

You have been hurt over time by people and situations. Sometimes, it seems so unfair and unjust. Life has thrown its share of curve balls and obstructions, but the good report is – You made it! Despite everything you experienced, the Lord brought you through.

The faces and memories of people who have hurt us come to mind when our thoughts are on forgiveness. No one likes to feel unjustly treated, violated or manipulated. It's cruel and insensitive, and it hurts us to our core.

The same way we do not want to disappoint our family members, friends, co-workers and neighbors, we should concern ourselves with not breaking the promises or covenants we made to the Lord.

Remember that forgiveness is a process. You may not forget what took place, but over time, the strength of the hurt will diminish. It does not mean to place yourself in the same position again. Instead, it means to make a choice to live in freedom and joy for the remainder of your days.

You have sinned. Sometimes you sin by choice and other times by failing to do something you should. Today, purify your life before Almighty God by simply admitting your faults, asking for forgiveness and making the promise to never repeat the error again.

Likewise, Jesus exhorts us to exercise forgiveness so we can be forgiven by God. Regardless of who has hurt you, begin the process to release them right now. I know it can hurt and I know you endured a lot, but you cannot allow the burden of unforgiveness to imprison you. Let go of the hurt and trust God to heal your pain. Your sins by omission and commission have directly affected your walk with the Lord.

You cannot move forward if your heart and spirit are focused on history.

The Lord has great plans for your life. When you hold on to pain, you are holding on to the past. You cannot move forward if your heart and spirit are focused on history. Your release of the person who wronged you does not justify their behavior or abolish their sentence for it. Instead, it allows you the privilege of atonement with the Lord.

Regardless of what mankind did to Him, the Lord Jesus showed love, care and forgiveness. Think about it–He forgave the ones who called for His demise, the one who betrayed Him, the one who denied Him, the many who doubted Him, liars, cheaters, idolaters, adulterers, murderers, fornicators, blasphemers and more. Even though He already knew what you would do, He died for you! The Lord Jesus' blood was shed on Calvary for your redemption and reconciliation with God.

After such an awesome sacrifice made for you, it would be a shame to allow something petty in comparison to separate you from a beautiful, eternal relationship and home in Heaven. Today is your opportunity to ensure you are in right relationship with God and others.

As you move in a new direction, the Lord is granting you new mercies. Amen!

Greater is coming!

Pastor D

BIBLICAL PASSAGES

Memory Verse: "Repent, then, and turn to God, so that your sins may be wiped out, that times of refreshing may come from the Lord" (Acts 3:19)."For if you forgive men when they sin against you, your heavenly Father will also forgive you. But if you do not forgive men their sins, your Father will not forgive your sins" (Matthew 6:14-15).

"Bear with each other and forgive one another if any of you has a grievance against someone. Forgive as the Lord forgave you" (Colossians 3:13).

"Get rid of all bitterness, rage and anger, brawling and slander, along with every form of malice. Be kind and compassionate to one another, forgiving each other, just as in Christ God forgave you" (Ephesians 4:31-32).

"Then Peter came to Jesus and asked, 'Lord, how many times shall I forgive my brother when he sins against me? Up to seven times?' Jesus answered, 'I tell you, not seven times, but seventy-seven times'" (Matthew 18:21-22).

"If anyone has caused grief, he has not so much grieved me as he has grieved all of you to some extent—not to put it too severely. The punishment inflicted on him by the majority is sufficient. Now instead, you ought to forgive and comfort him, so that he will not be overwhelmed by excessive sorrow. I urge you, therefore, to reaffirm your love for him" (2 Corinthians 2:5-8).

"Love is patient, love is kind. It does not envy, it does not boast, it is not proud. It does not dishonor others, it is not self-seeking, it is not easily angered, it keeps no record of wrongs. Love does not delight in evil but rejoices with the truth" (1 Corinthians 13:4-6).

"Therefore, if you are offering your gift at the altar and there remember that your brother has something against you, leave your gift there in front of the altar. First go and be reconciled to your brother; then come and offer your gift" (Matthew 5:23-24).

"Do not judge, and you will not be judged. Do not condemn, and you will not be condemned. Forgive, and you will be forgiven" (Luke 6:37).

"When they kept on questioning him, he straightened up and said to them, 'If any one of you is without sin, let him be the first to throw a stone at her'" (John 8:7).

"While they were stoning him, Stephen prayed, 'Lord Jesus, receive my spirit.' Then he fell on his knees and cried out, 'Lord, do not hold this sin against them.' When he had said this, he fell asleep" (Acts 7:59-60).

"When they came to a place called the Skull, there they crucified him, along with the criminals – one on his right, the other on his left, Jesus said, 'Father, forgive them, for they do not know what they are doing'" (Luke 23:33-34).

"So watch yourselves. If your brother sins, rebuke him, and if he repents forgive him. If he sins against you seven times in a day, and seven times comes back to you and says, 'I repent,' forgive him" (Luke 17:3-4).

"On the contrary: If your enemy is hungry, feed him; if he is thirsty, give him something to drink. In doing this, you will heap burning coals on his head" (Romans 12:20).

PERSONAL ASSESSMENT

Please check the following areas where you need forgiveness from the Lord. Then, pray the following prayer for each individual area: *"Lord, I confess to _____ in my life. Please forgive me and cleanse me in the name of Jesus. Amen"*

- Lying
- Stealing
- Abortion
- Murder
- Deception
- Manipulation
- Failing to tithe
- Drugs
- Bad attitude
- Excessive spending
- Overeating
- Displaced priorities
- Failure to support children
- Infidelity
- Adultery
- Fornication
- Bigamy
- Gossip
- Demeaning others
- Cursing God

- Hoarding things
- Unjust treatment
- Womanizer behavior
- Male bashing
- Greedy behavior
- Cursing others
- Hatred
- Fear
- Rape
- Molestation
- Drug use
- Pain
- Affliction
- Sexual perversion
- Pornography
- Jealousy
- Sensationalism
- Evil thoughts
- Suicide planning

LIFE TRANSFORMATION MESSAGE

A vital yet often challenging aspect of our Christian walk is forgiveness. Forgiveness is not a one-time act but a continuous process that requires our commitment and faith. It is essential for our spiritual, emotional, and relational health. Let us explore why forgiveness is so important and how we can embrace it as an ongoing journey in our lives.

> ———†———
>
> Forgiveness is not a one-time act but a continuous process that requires our commitment and faith.

Forgiveness is not merely a suggestion but a command from God. In Matthew 6:14-15, Jesus instructs the disciples and others, "For if you forgive other people when they sin against you, your heavenly Father will also forgive you. But if you do not forgive others their sins, your Father will not forgive your sins." This command underscores the gravity of forgiveness in our relationship with God. Our willingness to forgive others reflects our understanding and acceptance of God's forgiveness toward us.

Furthermore, our Lord Jesus provides the ultimate example of forgiveness. On the cross, despite immense suffering, He prayed, "Father, forgive them, for they do not know what they are doing" (Luke 23:34). Jesus' example shows us that forgiveness is possible even in the most painful circumstances. By following His example, we learn to extend grace and mercy to those who have wronged us, mirroring the grace we have received from Him.

As Christians, we resist this important part of our Christian walk because of inaccurate expectations associated with forgiveness. Forgiveness is a process, not a one-time event. It involves acknowledging the hurt, processing our emotions, and gradually letting go of resentment. Ephesians 4:31-32 advises, "Get rid of all bitterness, rage and anger, brawling and slander, along with every form of malice. Be kind and compassionate to one another, forgiving each other, just as in Christ God forgave you." This passage highlights the ongoing effort required to rid ourselves of negative emotions and embrace a forgiving heart.

Forgiveness liberates us from the bondage of bitterness and resentment. Holding onto grudges consumes our energy and hinders our spiritual growth. Hebrews 12:15 warns, "See to it that no one falls short of the grace of God and that no bitter root grows up to cause trouble and defile many." By forgiving, we uproot bitterness and make room for God's peace and joy in our hearts.

It is important to remember that forgiveness can open the door to reconciliation. While reconciliation requires the willingness of both parties, forgiveness paves the way for healing broken relationships. Romans 12:18 advises, "If it is possible, as far as it depends on you, live at peace with everyone." Our responsibility is to forgive and seek peace, even if the other person is not yet ready to reconcile. Remember you are responsible for your actions, while others are accountable for their actions.

Forgiveness can be challenging, but with God's help, it is possible. Here are some practical steps:

- Pray for the Strength to Forgive: Ask God to soften your heart and give you the strength to forgive.

- Acknowledge the Hurt: Be honest about your feelings and the pain caused.

- Let Go of Resentment: Choose to release feelings of anger and resentment, even if it takes time.

- Seek Support: Share your journey with trusted friends, a pastor, or a counselor who can provide guidance and encouragement.

- Remember God's Forgiveness: Reflect on the forgiveness you have received from God and let it inspire you to forgive others.

Dear friends, forgiveness is a powerful and transformative process. It requires our commitment and reliance on God's grace. By embracing forgiveness, we obey God's command, follow Jesus' example, and experience freedom from bitterness. Let us commit to the ongoing journey of forgiveness, trusting that God will heal our hearts and restore our relationships.

———†———

By embracing forgiveness, we obey God's command, follow Jesus' example, and experience freedom from bitterness.

May we be known as people of grace, compassion, and forgiveness, reflecting the love of Christ in all we do. Amen.

PERSONAL TRANSFORMATION ASSIGNMENT

1. Write a list of people that have wronged you. Then, pray and say aloud, *"I forgive you in the name of Jesus"* as you cross their name off the list. This week, make a call or send a message to that person and tell them, "I learned so much from our experiences together and I pray the best in your life." Thank God for freedom!

   _____

   _____

2. Read the following scriptures and write them in your own words. Ask the Holy Spirit to give you fresh revelation from these verses – Matthew 6:14-15; 1 John 1:9; Isaiah 43:25-26

   _____

   _____

3. Make a call or send a message to the persons you listed in question #1 and tell them, "I am grateful that our experiences in the past have equipped us for the future. My prayers are with you for a future of prosperity and power in the name of Jesus."

   _____

   _____

4. Write a "thank you' prayer to the Lord for the freedom you will experience.

   _____

   _____

5. Name a biblical character who forgave someone else. Write the scriptural reference.

   _____

   _____

6. What similarities do you have with this biblical character?

_____

_____

7. What has been the most difficult part of this lesson today?

_____

_____

8. How would you advise a new believer on how to forgive a spouse that committed adultery?

_____

_____

9. What sin does God hate?

_____

_____

10. Write your own statement that releases a person and offers forgiveness.

_____

_____

PRAYER

Dear Holy God,

Thank you for the gift of forgiveness and restoration. Please cleanse me of all guilt, shame and pain in the name of Jesus. Strengthen me now to walk with a new perspective and power. Amen!

JOURNAL ENTRY

(Please use this space or your own book designated for this time.)

The Lord has forgiven me for

_____

_____

_____

_____

I have forgiven myself for

_____

_____

_____

_____

I have forgiven others for

_____

_____

_____

_____

This prayer journey will help me to

_____

_____

_____

_____

"Sometimes you've got to let everything go–purge yourself.
If you are unhappy with anything... whatever is bringing you down,
get rid of it. Because you'll find that when you're free,
your true creativity, your true self comes out."

Tina Turner

Day Four

Word for the day: **PURGE**

My friend, you are making great strides in the 21 Days of Personal Transformation. You are rooted on the proper path, your prayer life is improving, and you have been cleansed of all sin and unrighteousness. The Lord is preparing you for great and mighty things!

Today, our focus is on the people and situations we are carrying with us. This will not be an easy exercise, but you can no longer allow dead weight to keep you from flying high. It's your time and season to realize goals and maximize potential. Advance – the kingdom of God awaits.

Greater is coming!

Pastor D

BIBLICAL PASSAGES

Memory Verse: "Purge me with hyssop, and I shall be clean: wash me, and I shall be whiter than snow" (Psalm 51:7 KJV).

"Therefore I, a prisoner for serving the Lord, beg you to lead a life worthy of your calling, for you have been called by God. Be humble and gentle. Be patient with each other, making allowance for each other's faults because of your love. Always keep yourselves united in the Holy Spirit, and bind yourselves together with peace. We are all one body, we have the same Spirit, and we have all been called to the same glorious future. There is only one Lord, one faith, one baptism, and there is only one God and Father, who is over us all and in us all and living through us all. However, he has given each one of us a special gift according to the generosity of Christ. That is why the Scriptures say, 'When he ascended to the heights, he led a crowd of captives and gave gifts to his people.' Notice that it says 'he ascended.' This means that Christ first came down to the lowly world in which we live. The same one who came down is the one who ascended higher than all the heavens, so that his rule might fill the entire universe. He is the one who gave these gifts to the church: the apostles, the prophets, the evangelists, and the pastors and teachers. Their responsibility is to equip God's people to do his work and build up the church, the body of Christ, until we come to such unity in our faith and knowledge of God's Son that we will be mature and full grown in the Lord, measuring up to the full stature of Christ. Then we will no longer be like children, forever changing our minds about what we believe because someone has told us something different or because someone has cleverly lied to us and made the lie sound like the truth. Instead, we will hold to the truth in love, becoming more and more in every way like Christ, who is the head of his body, the church. Under his direction, the whole body is fitted together perfectly. As each part does its own special work, it helps the other parts grow, so that the whole body is healthy and growing and full of love. With the Lord's authority let me say this: Live no longer as the ungodly do, for they are hopelessly confused. Their closed minds are full of darkness; they are far away from the life of God because they have shut their minds and hardened their hearts against him. They don't care anymore about right and wrong, and they have given themselves over to immoral ways. Their lives are filled with all kinds of impurity and greed. But that isn't what you were taught when you learned about Christ. Since you have heard all about him and have learned the truth that is in Jesus, throw off your old evil nature and your former way of life, which is rotten through and through, full of lust and deception. Instead, there must be a spiritual renewal of your thoughts and attitudes. You must display a new nature because you are a new person, created in God's likeness — righteous, holy, and true. So put away all falsehood and 'tell your neighbor the truth' because we belong to each other. And 'don't sin by letting anger gain control over you.' Don't let the sun go down while you are still angry, for anger gives a mighty foothold to the Devil. If you are a thief, stop stealing. Begin using your hands for honest work, and then give generously to others in need. Don't use foul or abusive language. Let everything you say be good and helpful, so that your words will be an encouragement to those who hear them. And do not bring sorrow to God's Holy Spirit by the way you live. Remember, he is the one who has identified you as his own, guaranteeing that you will be saved on the day of redemption. Get rid of all bitterness, rage, anger, harsh words, and slander, as well as all types of malicious behavior. Instead, be kind to each other, tenderhearted, forgiving one another, just as God through Christ has forgiven you" (Ephesians 4 NLT).

"I can hardly believe the report about the sexual immorality going on among you, something so evil that even the pagans don't do it. I am told that you have a man in your church who is living in sin with his father's wife. And you are so proud of yourselves! Why aren't you mourning in sorrow and shame? And why haven't you removed this man from your fellowship? Even though I am not there with you in person, I am with you in the Spirit. Concerning the one who has done this, I have already passed judgment in the name of the Lord Jesus. You are to call a meeting of the church, and I will be there in spirit, and the power of the Lord Jesus will be with you as you meet. Then you must cast this man out of the church and into Satan's hands, so that his sinful nature will be destroyed and he himself will be saved when the Lord returns. How terrible that you should boast about your spirituality, and yet you let this sort of thing go on. Don't you realize that if even one person is allowed to go on sinning, soon all will be affected? Remove this wicked person from among you so that you can stay pure. Christ, our Passover Lamb, has been sacrificed for us. So let us celebrate the festival, not by eating the old bread of wickedness and evil, but by eating the new bread of purity and truth. When I wrote to you before, I told you not to associate with people who indulge in sexual sin. But I wasn't talking about unbelievers who indulge in sexual sin, or who are greedy or are swindlers or idol worshipers. You would have to leave this world to avoid people like that. What I meant was that you are not to associate with anyone who claims to be a Christian yet indulges in sexual sin, or is greedy, or worships idols, or is abusive, or a drunkard, or a swindler. Don't even eat with such people. It isn't my responsibility to judge out-siders, but it certainly is your job to judge those inside the church who are sinning in these ways. God will judge those on the outside; but as the Scriptures say, 'You must remove the evil person from among you'" (1 Corinthians 5).

PERSONAL ASSESSMENT

1. Write down the things in your life that are not pleasing to God.

   _____

   _____

2. Name the people in your life that are not operating on the same faith level and/or not heading in the same direction that you are currently.

   _____

   _____

3. List the areas of your life that you are not pleased with personally and state why you are displeased in those areas.

   _____

   _____

LIFE TRANSFORMATION MESSAGE

Today, let us delve into the profound power of forgiveness and letting go. Forgiveness is a divine gift that liberates us from the chains of resentment and bitterness, allowing us to experience true freedom and healing. In Colossians 3:13, we are reminded, "Bear with each other and forgive one another if any of you has a grievance against someone. Forgive as the Lord forgave you." Just as we have been forgiven by God, so, too, are we called to extend forgiveness to others.

Forgiveness does not excuse the wrongdoing or justify the hurt inflicted upon us, but rather, it releases us from the burden of carrying the weight of anger and pain. When we choose to forgive, we break the cycle of retaliation and vengeance and open ourselves to the transformative power of love and reconciliation.

> When we choose to forgive, we break the cycle of retaliation and vengeance and open ourselves to the transformative power of love and reconciliation.

Moreover, forgiveness is not just for the benefit of the one who receives it, but also for the one who gives it. In Matthew 6:14-15, Jesus teaches us, "For if you forgive other people when they sin against you, your heavenly Father will also forgive you. But if you do not forgive others their sins, your Father will not forgive your sins." Forgiveness is an act of obedience to God's commandments, and it is through extending grace to others that we ourselves receive God's grace.

Letting go is closely intertwined with forgiveness, for it is through letting go that we release the grip of the past and embrace the possibilities of the present and future. In Isaiah 43:18-19, we are reminded, "Forget the former things; do not dwell on the past. See, I am doing a new thing! Now it springs up; do you not perceive it?" Letting go of past hurts,

> Letting go of past hurts, disappointments, and regrets allows us to make room for the new beginnings and blessings that God has in store for us.

disappointments, and regrets allows us to make room for the new beginnings and blessings that God has in store for us.

In 1998, I dedicated my life to international missions and I traveled as an international evangelist to South Africa. I packed three big bags full of books, clothes and supplies. When I arrived at the airport, the airline attendant informed me that I could only take two bags and both had to weigh 60 pounds or less. I had five minutes to shed 80 pounds! I learned at that moment – You must be careful what you take on assignment! Everything and everyone will not be able to travel with you to the next destination.

It was not easy unpacking and repacking, especially under pressure, but I had to lighten the load for the assignment. Similarly, there are some people, concerns and issues that we've been carrying with us from place to place. They crowd your space, distract you from your purpose and cause continual conflict. This is the last day for this to be your story.

As you prepare for the greatest breakthrough in your life's history, it is time to **LET IT GO**. You may cry for a moment, hear some negative words or suffer emotional pain, but the suffering is nothing compared to the glory that will be released in your life. Today, ask the Lord for direction and dismiss anything and anyone from the journey who is not permitted. Excess baggage will slow you down. It's time to propel into divine destiny!

As we journey through life, we will inevitably encounter moments of pain and betrayal, but we have the choice to respond with forgiveness and letting go. Let us heed the words of Ephesians 4:31-32, "Get rid of all bitterness, rage and anger, brawling and slander, along with every form of malice. Be kind and compassionate to one another, forgiving each other, just as in Christ God forgave you."

May we embrace the power of forgiveness and letting go, knowing that in doing so, we reflect the love and grace of our merciful God. Amen.

PERSONAL TRANSFORMATION ASSIGNMENT

1. Pray specifically about your character and attitude. Ask God to reveal the attributes that must be purged this year. Write them down for reference.

   _____

   _____

2. How has your excess baggage affected your past?

   _____

   _____

3. What will you do to ensure that the same issues, situations and people do not affect your future in the same manner?

   _____

   _____

4. What is the hardest part of letting go?

   _____

   _____

5. How will you release the excess baggage during this journey?

   _____

   _____

6. Name a biblical character that purged people and things from their life.

   _____

   _____

7. What have you learned from their story that you can apply to your own life?

_____

_____

8. James was a drug dealer and a pimp before he accepted the gift of salvation. Now, he wants to share this with his friends, but they are trying to pull him back into former things. What suggestions would you give James to stay on the proper path?

_____

_____

9. How will you stay on the proper path?

_____

_____

10. Write an acronym for PURGE

_____

_____

PRAYER

Dear Lord, I thank you for your purpose and plan in my life. Please purge all excess baggage and release me to do your will uninhibited, in the name of Jesus, Amen.

JOURNAL ENTRY

(Please use this space or your own book designated for this time.)

My excess baggage is

_____

_____

_____

_____

I'm laying aside

_____

_____

_____

_____

I am moving forward to

_____

_____

_____

_____

Today, I have been transformed by

_____

_____

_____

_____

"Keep your heart pure. A pure heart is necessary
to see God in each other. If you see God in each other,
there is love for each other, then there is peace."

~ Mother Teresa

Day Five

Word for the day: **PURE HEART**

Dear Journey Partner,

By now, I know you are experiencing some of the effects of the journey. You can travel lighter because you have shed excess baggage and your path is clearer than ever before. Take one moment and thank the Lord for all that is happening in your life. Hallelujah!

Today, our focus is on our hearts. In order to be successful in business, ministry, family development, etc. – our hearts must be pure. Today, evaluate your motives and make changes to be a better servant for the Lord.

Greater is coming!

Pastor D

BIBLICAL PASSAGES

Memory Verse: "God blesses those whose hearts are pure, for they will see God" (Matthew 5:8).

"The earth is the LORD's, and everything in it. The world and all its people belong to him. For he laid the earth's foundation on the seas and built it on the ocean depths. Who may climb the mountain of the LORD? Who may stand in his holy place? Only those whose hands and hearts are pure, who do not worship idols and never tell lies. They will receive the LORD's blessing and have right standing with God their savior. They alone may enter God's presence and worship the God of Israel. Interlude Open up, ancient gates! Open up, ancient doors, and let the King of glory enter. Who is the King of glory? The LORD, strong and mighty, the LORD, invincible in battle. Open up, ancient gates! Open up, ancient doors, and let the King of glory enter. Who is the King of glory? The LORD Almighty — he is the King of glory" (Psalm 32).

"Wine produces mockers; liquor leads to brawls. Whoever is led astray by drink cannot be wise. The king's fury is like a lion's roar; to rouse his anger is to risk your life. Avoiding a fight is a mark of honor; only fools insist on quarreling. If you are too lazy to plow in the right season, you will have no food at the harvest. Though good advice lies deep within a person's heart, the wise will draw it out. Many will say they are loyal friends, but who can find one who is really faithful? The godly walk with integrity; blessed are their children after them. When a king judges, he carefully weighs all the evidence, distinguishing the bad from the good. Who can say, 'I have cleansed my heart; I am pure and free from sin'? The LORD despises double standards of every kind. Even children are known by the way they act, whether their conduct is pure and right. Ears to hear and eyes to see — both are gifts from the LORD. If you love sleep, you will end in poverty. Keep your eyes open, and there will be plenty to eat! The buyer haggles over the price, saying, 'It's worthless,' then brags about getting a bargain! Wise speech is rarer and more valuable than gold and rubies. Be sure to get collateral from anyone who guarantees the debt of a stranger. Get a deposit if someone guarantees the debt of a foreigner. Stolen bread tastes sweet, but it turns to gravel in the mouth. Plans succeed through good counsel; don't go to war without the advice of others. A gossip tells secrets, so don't hang around with someone who talks too much. If you curse your father or mother, the lamp of your life will be snuffed out. An inheritance obtained early in life is not a blessing in the end. Don't say, 'I will get even for this wrong.' Wait for the LORD to handle the matter. The LORD despises double standards; he is not pleased by dishonest scales. How can we understand the road we travel? It is the LORD who directs our steps. It is dangerous to make a rash promise to God before counting the cost. A wise king finds the wicked, lays them out like wheat, then runs the crushing wheel over them. The LORD's searchlight penetrates the human spirit, exposing every hidden motive. Unfailing love and faithfulness protect the king; his throne is made secure through love. The glory of the young is their strength; the gray hair of experience is the splendor of the old. Physical punishment cleanses away evil; such discipline purifies the heart" (Proverbs 20).

PERSONAL ASSESSMENT

1. What is a pure heart?

   _____

   _____

2. Do you have a pure heart?

   _____

   _____

3. What is pure about your heart?

   _____

   _____

4. What is not pure about your heart?

   _____

   _____

5. What change do you need in your heart?

   _____

   _____

6. What will you do to activate transformation in your life?

   _____

   _____

LIFE TRANSFORMATION MESSAGE

In the last few days, you have earnestly prayed, sought God's pardon and purged things from your lives. Now, it's time to ensure that you have a pure heart to be successful all the days of your lives.

The condition of your heart determines your outcome in life. It is so important that as believers, we must judge our hearts to make sure we have motives that are pure and holy. James chapter 5 references prayers that remain unanswered because motives and intentions are not pure. It is paramount that you are cleansed and you ensure that your priorities and pursuits originate from a pure heart.

_____+_____

The condition of your heart determines your outcome in life.

_____

The writings within Psalm 24 reminds us of the importance of a pure heart because it enables a person to experience the blessings of the Lord. Also, in the Gospel, Matthew 5 reminds us that we will see God when our hearts are pure. There are blessings you will not receive if your heart is not pure. I encourage you not to allow anyone or anything to separate you from the blessed life the Lord is preparing you to live.

To receive a pure heart, you must repent of all past sins and errors. Remember, the difference between forgiveness and repentance – with repentance, you are promising not to repeat the same sin again. Also, ask God for internal cleansing and to make you more like God each day. Afterward, you must have heart maintenance on a consistent basis.

How do you maintain a pure heart?

1. Ask God daily to cleanse you of all sin and unrighteousness.
2. Continually evaluate your life and purge negative attitudes and behaviors from your character and environment.
3. Be careful who you allow to speak into your life!
4. Guard your heart by reading and meditating on the scriptures daily.

5. In a moment of trial, do not speak first. Take time to reflect and evaluate the situation. Then, make sure your responses are done in a spirit of love.
6. Be careful to rid your spirit of all contaminations immediately.
7. Ask for forgiveness often and offer forgiveness to others more often.

Today, please guard your heart against anyone or anything that will contaminate your heart. You have come too far in the journey to allow anything to prevent the realization of your goals, visions and dreams. Ask the Lord to cultivate a clean heart in you and maintain that pure heart for your journey.

PERSONAL TRANSFORMATION ASSIGNMENT

1. Read Psalm 51:10-11. Write down your interpretation of that scripture and how it applies to your life presently.

    _____

    _____

2. What has separated your heart from God?

    _____

    _____

3. What will you do to ensure that your heart is pure today?

    _____

    _____

4. Read 2 Timothy 2:22 and write how it applies to your present life situation.

    _____

    _____

5. Research one biblical character that had a pure heart. Write down at least three personal characteristics or attributes about that person.

    _____

    _____

6. What part of heart maintenance is easiest for you?

    _____

    _____

7. What part of heart maintenance is most difficult for you?

    _____

    _____

8. Write down a personal testimony of how God has changed your heart.

_____

_____

9. Share your personal testimony with at least two other people today. Write down their names here.

_____

_____

10. Write yourself a word of encouragement for this journey.

_____

_____

PRAYER

Lord, please purify my heart that I may look, act and think like Jesus. Amen.

JOURNAL ENTRY

(Please use this space or your own book designated for this time.)

In the past, my heart was

_____

_____

_____

_____

Today, my heart's condition is

_____

_____

_____

_____

I will maintain my pure heart by

_____

_____

_____

_____

Today, I have been transformed by

_____

_____

_____

_____

I come to the garden alone,
While the dew is still on the roses,
And the voice I hear falling on my ear
The Son of God discloses. -

Refrain:
And He walks with me, and He talks with me,
And He tells me I am His own;
And the joy we share as we tarry there,
None other has ever known.

He speaks, and the sound of His voice
Is so sweet the birds hush their singing,
And the melody that He gave to me
Within my heart is ringing.

I'd stay in the garden with Him,
Though the night around me be falling,
But He bids me go; through the voice of woe
His voice to me is calling.

Charles Miles, 1913

Day Six

Word for the day: **PRESENCE OF GOD**

Dear Journey Partner,

With a pure heart and a renewed focus, it is time to move forward with the visions, dreams and goals the Lord has given you. How do you move forward? You must listen to the direction of the Lord, which is given directly to you in God's holy presence. Spend intimate time with God today and for the remainder of this journey, as God unfolds great and mighty promises and revelations. Remember, everything you face in your life today is in God's hands, so stand still and focus on your relationship with the Lord. Matthew 6:33 reminds us that when you seek God first, ALL the other things will be added to you.

As we begin a new day, let us take a moment to reflect on the importance of being in the presence of God. In the hustle and bustle of our daily lives, it can be easy to get caught up in our own thoughts and worries, but it is crucial to remember the value of spending time with our Creator.

Being in the presence of God allows us to find peace and strength in the midst of chaos. It is a time to quiet our minds and open our hearts to God's love and guidance. When we intentionally seek God's presence, we invite God to work in our lives and to lead us on the path that has been set before us.

In the presence of God, we find comfort and reassurance. We are reminded of God's faithfulness and God's promises, and we are filled with a sense of hope and purpose. It is in God's presence that we can lay down our burdens and find rest for our souls.

Let us not underestimate the power of spending time with God each morning. It is in these moments that we can align our hearts with God's will and seek God's direction for the day ahead. As we go about our daily activities, let us carry with us the peace and strength that comes from being in God's presence.

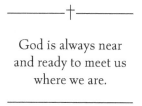

God is always near and ready to meet us where we are.

May we seek God's presence with intention and fervor, knowing that God is always near and ready to meet us where we are. Go to your quiet space now and bask in the presence of the Lord today. It's your time and season for personal transformation.

Greater is coming!

Pastor D

BIBLICAL PASSAGES

Memory Verse: "The Lord your God is in your midst, a mighty one who will save; he will rejoice over you with gladness; he will quiet you by his love; he will exult over you with loud singing" (Zephaniah 3:17).

"Keep me safe, O God, for I have come to you for refuge. I said to the LORD, 'You are my Master! All the good things I have are from you.' The godly people in the land are my true heroes! I take pleasure in them! Those who chase after other gods will be filled with sorrow. I will not take part in their sacrifices or even speak the names of their gods. LORD, you alone are my inheritance, my cup of blessing. You guard all that is mine. The land you have given me is a pleasant land. What a wonderful inheritance! I will bless the LORD who guides me; even at night my heart instructs me. I know the LORD is always with me. I will not be shaken, for he is right beside me. No wonder my heart is filled with joy, and my mouth shouts his praises! My body rests in safety. For you will not leave my soul among the dead or allow your godly one to rot in the grave. You will show me the way of life, granting me the joy of your presence and the pleasures of living with you forever" (Psalm 16). "The LORD said to Moses, 'Now that you have brought these people out of Egypt, lead them to the land I solemnly promised Abraham, Isaac, and Jacob. I told them long ago that I would give this land to their descendants. And I will send an angel before you to drive out the Canaanites, Amorites, Hittites, Perizzites, Hivites, and Jebusites. Theirs is a land flowing with milk and honey. But I will not travel along with you, for you are a stubborn, unruly people. If I did, I would be tempted to destroy you along the way.' When the people heard these stern words, they went into mourning and refused to wear their jewelry and ornaments. For the LORD had told Moses to tell them, 'You are an unruly, stubborn people. If I were there among you for even a moment, I would destroy you. Remove your jewelry and ornaments until I decide what to do with you.' So from the time they left Mount Sinai, the Israelites wore no more jewelry. It was Moses' custom to set up the tent known as the Tent of

Meeting far outside the camp. Everyone who wanted to consult with the LORD would go there. Whenever Moses went out to the Tent of Meeting, all the people would get up and stand in their tent entrances. They would all watch Moses until he disappeared inside. As he went into the tent, the pillar of cloud would come down and hover at the entrance while the LORD spoke with Moses. Then all the people would stand and bow low at their tent entrances. Inside the Tent of Meeting, the LORD would speak to Moses face to face, as a man speaks to his friend. Afterward Moses would return to the camp, but the young man who assisted him, Joshua son of Nun, stayed behind in the Tent of Meeting. Moses said to the LORD, 'You have been telling me, Take these people up to the Promised Land. But you haven't told me whom you will send with me. You call me by name and tell me I have found favor with you. Please, if this is really so, show me your intentions so I will understand you more fully and do exactly what you want me to do. Besides, don't forget that this nation is your very own people.' And the LORD replied, 'I will personally go with you, Moses. I will give you rest — everything will be fine for you.' Then Moses said, 'If you don't go with us personally, don't let us move a step from this place. If you don't go with us, how will anyone ever know that your people and I have found favor with you? How else will they know we are special and distinct from all other people on the earth?' And the LORD replied to Moses, 'I will indeed do what you have asked, for you have found favor with me, and you are my friend.' Then Moses had one more request. 'Please let me see your glorious presence,' he said. The LORD replied, 'I will make all my goodness pass before you, and I will call out my name, 'the LORD,' to you. I will show kindness to anyone I choose, and I will show mercy to anyone I choose. But you may not look directly at my face, for no one may see me and live.' The LORD continued, 'Stand here on this rock beside me. As my glorious presence passes by, I will put you in the cleft of the rock and cover you with my hand until I have passed. Then I will remove my hand, and you will see me from behind. But my face will not be seen'" (Exodus 33).

PERSONAL ASSESSMENT

1. Where is the presence of God?

   _____

   _____

2. Have you ever been in the presence of God? Elaborate on your answer.

   _____

   _____

3. What must you do before you enter into God's presence?

   _____

   _____

4. What are the similarities between you and Moses?

   _____

   _____

5. What are the differences between you and Moses?

   _____

   _____

6. What will you do today to activate more transformation in your life?

   _____

   _____

LIFE TRANSFORMATION MESSAGE

There is nothing like being in the presence of Almighty God. It is a transformational experience, and we grow from the time and glory of the Lord. As Christians, there are times in our lives that we may not feel as close to the Lord, and we need to focus on God and sense God's holy presence. Trials and tragedies in life will cause you to feel alone and abandoned, but there are ways to re-focus and experience the constant presence of the Lord. Remember, God is always near you and when you need to re-focus, please take time to do the following:

1. **Repent** – Sometimes you do not sense God's presence because there is something blocking your communication with the Lord. David experienced this in the Psalms and recorded these words: *"Then I acknowledged my sin to you and did not cover up my iniquity. I said I will confess my transgressions to the Lord and you forgave the guild of my sin."* 1 John 1:9 reminds us that God is faithful and just to forgive us and cleanse us of all unrighteousness. When there seems to be a block in communication, open your heart and let God cleanse you.

2. **Meditation** – Sometimes we do not hear clearly because of the hustle and bustle in life. We need to be quiet and listen! Spend some quiet, quality time reading the scriptures and just enjoying peace. The word of God will become alive to you as you study. "Be Still and Know that I am God" (Psalm 46:10).

3. **Sing to the Lord!** The Bible refers to our praise and singing as an opportunity to embrace the presence of God. The Lord inhabits the praises of His people; and He will make His presence known as you sing to Him.

4. **Praise the Lord** – Just utter the words "Hallelujah" and "Thank you, Jesus" over and over during your moments of adoration. Do not ask for anything, but give thanks for everything and honor God for divine attributes.

5. **Join with others in prayer and praise** – The Lord promised to be in the midst when two or three gather together in HIS name. Instead of shopping or having a dinner date, wouldn't it be wonderful to have a praise party? Invite others to join with you and seek the Lord.

When we seek the Lord, God will make the divine presence known to us. Today, make a promise that you will seek to feel the presence of the Lord each day of your life and spend time with God on a consistent basis.

———†———

Spend time with God on a consistent basis.

The visions and goals we wrote and prayed about during the early days of this journey can only be realized as you spend precious time with the Lord, allowing God to mold you and give direction for the future. Keep a journal by your side and record the many things that are deposited in your spirit.

I am excited that you are taking your life to the next level as you read, study, pray and seek the Lord. If you already spend ten minutes each day, increase to twenty and higher over time. As you demonstrate your faithfulness, God is preparing you for the time of exaltation.

Greater is coming!

PERSONAL TRANSFORMATION ASSIGNMENT

1. Read 1 Thessalonians 2:13-14. Write down your interpretation of that scripture and how it applies to your life presently.

   _____

   _____

2. What do you desire most from God?

   _____

   _____

3. How does God make His presence known to you?

   _____

   _____

4. Read Psalm 16:11 and write how it applies to your present life situation.

   _____

   _____

5. Research one biblical character that had a personal encounter with the Lord. Write down at least three personal characteristics or attributes about that person.

   _____

   _____

6. What part of re-focusing on the presence of the Lord is easiest for you?

   _____

   _____

7. What part of re-focusing on the presence of the Lord is most difficult for you?

_____

_____

8. Write a poem or song you will present to the Lord during times you do not sense His presence strongly.

_____

_____

9. What is the Lord leading you to amend in your relationship with God?

_____

_____

10. What advice and encouragement would you give to someone who has never had a personal one-on-one encounter with God?

_____

_____

PRAYER

Lord, please allow me to experience your presence in a greater way. Forgive me for all sins and anything that has impeded our communication. Please restore me now, and draw me closer to you, in the name of Jesus. Amen.

JOURNAL ENTRY

(Please use this space or your own book designated for this time.)

Lord, your presence

_____

_____

_____

_____

Today, I desire to

_____

_____

_____

_____

I will cultivate a closer relationship with the Lord by

_____

_____

_____

_____

Today, I have been transformed by

_____

_____

_____

_____

"There are two questions that we have to ask ourselves. The first is 'Where am I going?' and the second is 'Who will go with me?'"
Howard Thurman

"Use me, God. Show me how to take who I am, who I want to be, and what I can do, and use it for a purpose greater than myself."
Martin Luther King, Jr.

Day Seven

Word for the day: **PURPOSE**

Dear Journey Partner,

It's day #7! You are completing a full week of this personal transformation experience that will upgrade your life. Now that your heart, mind and spirit are in the right place, we will focus on your purpose in life. Your purpose is the reason you were born and the main thing that only you can accomplish for the kingdom. Your time, energy and resources should be used toward the fulfillment of your purpose. As you surrender, the Holy Spirit will make the directions clear, and show you how to navigate in the days to come. You are about to enter into new territory – Get ready!!

> ———✝———
>
> Your purpose is the reason you were born and the main thing that only you can accomplish for the kingdom.

Greater is coming!

Pastor D

BIBLICAL PASSAGES

Memory Verse: "The Lord will fulfill his purpose for me, your steadfast love, O Lord, endures forever. Do not forsake the work of your hands" (Psalm 138:8).

"Whatever you do, work heartily, as for the Lord, and not for me" (Colossians 3:23).

"For the vision awaits its appointed time, it hastens to the end – it will not lie. If it seems slow, wait for it, it will surely come; it will not delay" (Habakkuk 2:3).

"Where there is no counsel, purposes are frustrated, but with many counselors they are accomplished" (Proverbs 15:22).

"Many plans are in a man's mind, but it is the Lord's purpose for him that will stand" (Proverbs 19:21).

"And God purposed that through (by the service, the intervention of) Him [the Son] all things should be completely reconciled back to Himself, whether on earth or in heaven, as through Him, [the Father] made peace by means of the blood of His cross" (Colossians 1:20).

"Purposes and plans are established by counsel; and [only] with good advice make or carry on war" (Proverbs 20:18).

"Now to Him Who, by (in consequence of) the [action of His] power that is at work within us, is able to [carry out His purpose and] do superabundantly, far over and above all that we [dare] ask or think [infinitely beyond our highest prayers, desires, thoughts, hopes, or dreams]" (Ephesians 3:20).

"But for this very purpose have I let you live, that I might show you My power, and that My name may be declared throughout all the earth" (Exodus 9:16).

"The Lord of hosts has sworn, saying, Surely, as I have thought and planned, so shall it come to pass, and as I have purposed, so shall it stand" (Isaiah 14:24).

"O LORD, You are my God; I will exalt You, I will praise Your name, for You have done wonderful things, even purposes planned of old [and fulfilled] in faithfulness and truth" (Isaiah 25:1).

"For I know the thoughts and plans that I have for you, says the Lord, thoughts and plans for welfare and peace and not for evil, to give you hope in your final outcome" (Jeremiah 29:11).

"Let this same attitude and purpose and [humble] mind be in you which was in Christ Jesus: [Let Him be your example in humility:]" (Philippians 2:5).

"For I have come down from heaven not to do My own will and purpose but to do the will and purpose of Him Who sent Me" (John 6:38).

"For this is My Father's will and His purpose, that everyone who sees the Son and believes in and cleaves to and trusts in and relies on Him should have eternal life, and I will raise him up [from the dead] at the last day" (John 6:40).

"We are assured and know that [God being a partner in their labor] all things work together and are [fitting into a plan] for good to and for those who love God and are called according to [His] design and purpose" (Romans 8:28).

PERSONAL ASSESSMENT

1. Do you know your purpose in life?

   _____

   _____

2. What is your purpose?

   _____

   _____

3. How are you currently fulfilling your purpose? Why or why not?

   _____

   _____

4. What has distracted you from your purpose?

   _____

   _____

5. What breaks your heart when you hear about it?

   _____

   _____

6. How do you help advance the kingdom of God?

   _____

   _____

7. Do you believe that you should be accomplishing more in your life?

   _____

   _____

LIFE TRANSFORMATION MESSAGE

The Lord has a plan and purpose for each life and ensures that each person has gifts, skills and talents that make them unique. Only that person can fulfill their purpose in this life and world.

People with exceptional graces and purpose are often faced with personal attacks and tribulations in life. The adversary directly attacks personhood and purpose. If he can distract or detour you from advancement, the blessings for many lives will be hindered. That is why it is key to know your purpose and stay focused on fulfillment.

Your journey has been met by trial and tribulation every time you set out to accomplish goals, dreams, and visions. This is not a direct attack on you; it is a plot to keep you from fulfilling destiny. When you accomplish your aims, so many people will be blessed, fulfilled and changed. So, there is a fight to keep you from fulfilling your purpose. What should you do? Fight harder!

> When you accomplish your aims, so many people will be blessed, fulfilled and changed.

The race is not given to the swift or the strong, but to the one who endures to the end. There is a purpose for everything you have been through. There is a master plan. Today, please seek the Lord about your purpose.

Moses' purpose was leading God's people out of captivity. Esther's purpose was the salvation of her people. Sarah's purpose was to demonstrate the promise-keeping covenant of God. Mary's purpose was to birth a miracle. Jesus' purpose was atonement and redemption for mankind.

Each biblical character had to endure a momentary fight and obstruction in their path, but the Almighty prepared them for the promise and propelled them with power. Similarly, you will be fortified and enriched at each stage of your journey and the world will receive a blessing from your testimony.

There was a burden in my life. I was a victim of domestic violence and almost lost my life to someone's angry woes. Afterward, my heart would sink every time I saw a woman with a bruise or a child afraid because of the violence they experienced. That was my misery and it became my ministry. Now, I am able to minister around the world and help victims become survivors. As a result, I founded New Beginnings Foundation, a nonprofit that provides emergency aid and resources for domestic violence victims and families. Victims become victorious as a result of classes, counseling, clothing and other forms of assistance in our program.

I did not understand why God would allow me to experience such pain and turmoil, especially as someone who has dedicated my life to Christian service. However, I can now appreciate every experience because it properly prepared me for the work that I do now and the plans for the future. I learned to be empathetic, loving and gracious. Those are important attributes in helping others to reach a place of healing and personal growth in life. As I look back in retrospect, I would not take anything for my journey now. I am able to be an integral part in changing this world as a result of the demonstrated power to overcome in my life.

Similarly, you have experienced misery in areas of your life. God uses those moments to lead us to true purpose. You can aid others by using the gifts God has placed inside of you.

What is your calling? What do you do that brings you great satisfaction? What could you do all day and not become tired?

A friend shared a quote: "Find something that breaks your heart, then break your back to fix it. That's purpose – walk in it." Today, ask the Lord to reveal the true purpose for your life and future, so you can move forward by faith. Greater is coming!

PERSONAL TRANSFORMATION ASSIGNMENT

1. Read John 6:38. Write down your interpretation of that scripture and how it applies to your life presently.

   _____

   _____

2. What major situations have prepared you for this time in your life?

   _____

   _____

3. How did you grow from those experiences?

   _____

   _____

4. Read Romans 8:28 and write how it applies to your present life situation

   _____

   _____

5. Research one biblical character that had a similar experience in life. Write down how they overcame the issue and the outstanding facts about their life.

   _____

   _____

6. Write a personal purpose statement.
   a. (Example: I was born to help others in crisis. I give my time to ministering to domestic violence victims and encouraging them for the future.)

   _____

   _____

7. What part of this lesson has been easiest for you? Why?

   _____

   _____

8. What part of this lesson has been the most difficult for you? Why?

   _____

   _____

9. What were you born to do in your life? Are you fulfilling that presently? Why or why not?

   _____

   _____

10. What advice and encouragement would you give to someone who is trying to find their purpose in life?

    _____

    _____

PRAYER

Lord, please reveal my true purpose in life. Enable and equip me to walk in that purpose all of the days of my life. I pray in the name of Jesus. Amen.

JOURNAL ENTRY

(Please use this space or your own book designated for this time.)

The things that break my heart are

_____

_____

_____

_____

I am happiest when I

_____

_____

_____

_____

I want to spend the rest of my life

_____

_____

_____

_____

Today, I have been transformed by

_____

_____

_____

_____

"I suspect that God's plan, whatever it is, works on a scale too large to admit our mortal tribulations; that in a single lifetime, accidents and happenstance determine more than we care to admit; and that the best we can do is to try to align ourselves with what we feel is right and construct some meaning out of our confusion, and with grace and nerve play at each moment the hand that we're dealt."

— **Barack Obama, <u>A Promised Land</u>**

Day Eight

Word for the day: **PREPARATION**

Dear Journey Partner,

You have been engaged in the important soul work that leads to personal transformation. It has not been easy, but it is beneficial. Today, please pause and celebrate yourself for the great progress you have made and the achievements you are in route to accomplish. This is a time of dedication and celebration.

Now that you are making active steps to fulfill your true purpose, it is important to have a plan so you can adequately prepare for the future. To borrow a phrase that has blessed my life, "Plan to work and work your plan."

Greater is coming!

Pastor D

BIBLICAL PASSAGES

Memory Verse: "Prepare your work outside; get everything ready for yourself in the field, and after that build your house" (Proverbs 24:27).

"We can gather our thoughts, but the LORD gives the right answer. People may be pure in their own eyes, but the LORD examines their motives. Commit your work to the LORD, and then your plans will succeed. The LORD has made everything for his own purposes, even the wicked for punishment. The LORD despises pride; be assured that the proud will be punished. Unfailing love and faithfulness cover sin; evil is avoided by fear of the LORD. When the ways of people please the LORD, he makes even their enemies live at peace with them. It is better to be poor and godly than rich and dishonest. We can make our plans, but the LORD determines our steps" (Proverbs 16:1-9).

"Be dressed ready for service and keep your lamps burning, like men waiting for their master to return from a wedding banquet, so that when he comes and knocks, they can immediately open the door for him. It will be good for those servants whose master finds them watching when he comes. I tell you the truth, he will dress himself to serve, will have them recline at the table and will come and wait on them. It will be good for those servants whose master finds them ready, even if he comes in the second or third watch of the night. But understand this: If the owner of the house had known at what hour the thief was coming, he would not have let his house be broken into. You also must be ready, because the Son of Man will come at an hour when you do not expect him" (Luke 12:35-40).

"Our people must learn to devote themselves to doing what is good, in order that they may provide for daily necessities and not live unproductive lives" (Titus 3:14).

"The plans of the diligent lead to profit as surely as haste leads to poverty" (Proverbs 21:5).

"Plans fail for lack of counsel, but with many advisers they succeed". (Proverbs 15:22).

"Listen to advice and accept instruction, and in the end you will be wise."(Proverbs 19:20).

"The earth is the Lord's, and everything in it, the world, and all who live in it; for he founded it upon the seas and established it upon the waters" (Psalm 24:1,2).

"Many are the plans in a man's heart, but it is the Lord's purpose that prevails" (Proverbs 19:21).

"Consider carefully what you hear," he continued. "With the measure you use, it will be measured to you-and even more. Whoever has will be given more; whoever does not have, even what he has will be taken from him" (Mark 4:24,25).

PERSONAL ASSESSMENT

1. Who do you consult before you make a major decision? Why?

   _____

   _____

2. What things do you need to fulfill your purpose (i.e., education, money, staff, etc.)?

   _____

   _____

3. How will you attain these things?

   _____

   _____

4. Use the following timetable to show what you will accomplish each month of this year.

   _____

   _____

Month	Things to Accomplish toward Fulfilling Your Purpose
January	
February	
March	
April	
May	
June	
July	
August	
September	
October	
November	
December	

LIFE TRANSFORMATION MESSAGE

Our promises lead us through preparation into the successful achievement of personal plans. There is a direct connection between preparation and success. It is wonderful to know your purpose, but you must be certain that you are prepared to walk in your calling.

The Lord allowed you to endure times of tribulation in your life as you developed clear direction to your purpose and gained momentum towards your potential. It was not by chance but divine arrangement that you are in this present state of being and going through this time of transformation. This is your season and time to make a major thrust forward in your life. Now that you know your purpose and God's plan, we must seek divine direction for the accomplishment of such. How will these things come to fruition in your life?

After I accepted my calling to ministry in the 1990's, it was pertinent that I adequately prepared for such. I enrolled in the appropriate courses, had seasons of prayer and fasting and linked up with persons for mentoring and strength. There were other things in my life that I did alone, but it was quite clear that I needed the wisdom, love and support of others to prepare for my future.

—————✝—————

God leads us through a preparation phase for each vision, dream, goal, calling, stage and/or season of our lives.

—————————

Similarly, God leads us through a preparation phase for each vision, dream, goal, calling, stage and/or season of our lives. We must possess the proper knowledge, wisdom, support system, resources and commitment for plans to prosper.

I know you may become anxious and want to leap into the next stage and phase, but please continue to consult the Lord for divine direction and guidance in each step and learn to wait on God! Also, practical knowledge is essential. Read books, enroll in classes, study from someone who has already traveled in this pathway. Everyone needs a mentor. You are not expected to begin as a sage. This is a new season and the Lord will lead you through this unchartered territory.

In the prophetic book of Nehemiah 4, the word of God reveals the people were successful, despite obstacles and numerous adversaries because there was a plan. Some of the members of the army would provide protection while others did the physical work of rebuilding the wall. Verse six records, "The people had a mind to work." There must be a plan. Your success is contingent upon vision-casting, proper planning and relationship maintenance with the Lord.

The Lord has given you great visions and goals for your life. This cannot be accomplished without your willingness to work, be resourceful and to network. You cannot do it alone. Today, begin to ask the Lord to prepare you and others for the next stage of vision fulfillment in your life. Greater is coming!

PERSONAL TRANSFORMATION ASSIGNMENT

1. Read your personal purpose statement. Summarize it in three words.

   _____

   _____

2. Write down three goals to accomplish in the next year in the fulfillment of your purpose.

   _____

   _____

3. Write down three goals to accomplish in the next three years of your life in the fulfillment of your purpose.

   _____

   _____

4. Write down five goals to accomplish in the next five years of your life in the fulfillment of your purpose.

   _____

   _____

5. Write down five goals to accomplish in the next ten years of your life in the fulfillment of your purpose.

   _____

   _____

6. Research one biblical character that had obstacles in the course of fulfilling their journey. Write down three things they did in the process.

   _____

   _____

7. What part of this lesson has been easiest for you? Why?

_____

_____

8. What part of this lesson has been the most difficult for you? Why?

_____

_____

9. What preparation are you currently engaged in for the fulfillment of your purpose?

_____

_____

10. What new and exciting things will you pursue in this new season of your life?

_____

_____

PRAYER

Lord, I submit the plan to the fulfillment of my purpose. Ignite the excitement in me and put the proper support system in my pathway that your will shall be done in my life, in the name of Jesus. Amen.

JOURNAL ENTRY

(Please use this space or your own book designated for this time.)

Lord, I thank you for the plan to

_____

_____

_____

_____

Lord, please send people to

_____

_____

_____

_____

Lord, please bless

_____

_____

_____

_____

Today, I have been transformed by

_____

_____

_____

_____

"Success is not final, failure is not fatal:
It is the courage to continue that counts."

—Winston Churchill

Day Nine

<<<<<<<<<<<<<<<<<<<<<<<<<<<<<<<<<<<<<<<<<<<<<<<<<<<<<<<<<<<<<<

Word for the day: **PERSEVERANCE**

Dear Journey Partner,

We've made it to Day #9! This has been a time of progression and personal growth. There has been so much to think over, plan for and pray about each day. It can be overwhelming at times. Periodically, I encourage you to read back over previous days and mark your progress. Truly, these 21 days will drastically change your life for the better. This is a season of transformation and upgrade for you. Your life will never be the same again.

This is the day where your body needs an additional push and your spirit must be renewed. Don't give up – the rewards of your labor are too valuable! Reach out to your accountability partner or a trusted individual today and trust God to make it through. The best is yet to come for you.

Greater is coming!

Pastor D

BIBLICAL PASSAGES

Memory Verse: "Patience endurance is what you need now, so that you will continue to do God's will. Then, you will receive all that he as promised" (Hebrews 10:36 NLT).

"Comfort, comfort my people," says your God. "Speak tenderly to Jerusalem. Tell her that her sad days are gone and that her sins are pardoned. Yes, the LORD has punished her in full for all her sins." Listen! I hear the voice of someone shouting, "Make a highway for the LORD through the wilderness. Make a straight, smooth road through the desert for our God. Fill the valleys and level the hills. Straighten out the curves and smooth off the rough spots. Then the glory of the LORD will be revealed, and all people will see it together. The LORD has spoken!" A voice said, "Shout!" I asked, "What should I shout?" "Shout that people are like the grass that dies away. Their beauty fades as quickly as the beauty of flowers in a field. The grass withers, and the flowers fade beneath the breath of the LORD. And so it is with people. The grass withers, and the flowers fade, but the word of our God stands forever." Messenger of good news, shout to Zion from the mountaintops! Shout louder to Jerusalem — do not be afraid. Tell the towns of Judah, "Your God is coming!" Yes, the Sovereign LORD is coming in all his glorious power. He will rule with awesome strength. See, he brings his reward with him as he comes. He will feed his flock like a shepherd. He will carry the lambs in his arms, holding them close to his heart. He will gently lead the mother sheep with their young. Who else has held the oceans in his hand? Who has measured off the heavens with his fingers? Who else knows the weight of the earth or has weighed out the mountains and the hills? Who is able to advise the Spirit of the LORD? Who knows enough to be his teacher or counselor? Has the LORD ever needed anyone's advice? Does he need instruction about what is good or what is best? No, for all the nations of the world are nothing in comparison with him. They are but a drop in the bucket, dust on the scales. He picks up the islands as though they had no weight at all. All Lebanon's forests do not contain sufficient fuel to consume a sacrifice large enough to honor him. All Lebanon's sacrificial animals would not make an offering worthy of our God. The nations of the world are as nothing to him. In his eyes they are less than nothing — mere emptiness and froth. To whom, then, can we compare God? What image might we find to resemble him? Can he be compared to an idol formed in a mold, overlaid with gold, and decorated with silver chains? Or is a poor person's wooden idol better? Can God be compared to an idol that must be placed on a stand, so it won't fall down? Have you never heard or understood? Are you deaf to the words of God — the words he gave before the world began? Are you so ignorant? It is God who sits above the circle of the earth. The people below must seem to him like grasshoppers! He is the one who spreads out the heavens like a curtain and makes his tent from them. He judges the great people of the world and brings them all to nothing. They hardly get started, barely taking root, when he blows on them and their work withers. The wind carries them off like straw. "To whom will you compare me? Who is my equal?" asks the Holy One. Look up into the heavens. Who created all the stars? He brings them out one after another, calling each by its name. And he counts them to see that none are lost or have strayed away. O Israel, how can you say the LORD does not see your troubles? How can you say God refuses to hear your case? Have you never heard or understood? Don't you know that the LORD is the everlasting God, the Creator of all the earth? He never grows faint or weary. No one can measure the depths of his understanding. He gives power to those who are tired and worn out; he offers strength to the weak. Even youths will become exhausted, and young men will give up. But those who wait on the LORD will find new strength. They will fly high on wings like eagles. They will run and not grow weary. They will walk and not faint" (Isaiah 40).

PERSONAL ASSESSMENT

1. How do you feel today?

    _____

    _____

2. What makes you tired, frustrated or disgruntled in a situation?

    _____

    _____

3. Do you give up easily? Why or why not?

    _____

    _____

4. How do you encourage yourself?

    _____

    _____

5. Who has God placed in your life as an encouragement and inspiration for you?

    _____

    _____

LIFE TRANSFORMATION MESSAGE

Life, as we all know, is a journey filled with escstatic moments, lessons, trials and tribulations, obstacles and challenges. Yet, it is through perseverance that we find the strength to endure, to overcome, and to emerge victoriously.

In the face of adversity, it is easy to feel overwhelmed, to doubt our abilities, and to succumb to despair. But remember, my beloved, that within each of us lies a wellspring of resilience waiting to be tapped into. It is in the darkest of moments that the light within us shines the brightest.

Perseverance is not simply about stubbornly refusing to give up; it is about summoning the courage to keep moving forward, even when the path ahead seems daunting. It is about finding the inner resolve to rise above our circumstances and to continue striving for our dreams and aspirations.

> Perseverance is not simply about stubbornly refusing to give up; it is about summoning the courage to keep moving forward, even when the path ahead seems daunting.

Think of the mighty oak tree, whose roots run deep and anchor it firmly to the earth. Despite the fiercest storms, it stands tall and unwavering, bending but never breaking. So, too, must we cultivate our inner strength, nurturing our spirits with faith, hope, and determination.

My dear friends, let us draw inspiration from those who have gone before us, from the countless individuals who have faced seemingly insurmountable odds and yet emerged triumphant. Their stories remind us that with perseverance, anything is possible.

> Perseverance is not the absence of struggle but rather the steadfastness of spirit in the face of adversity.

So, as you journey through life's ups and downs, remember these words: perseverance is not the absence of struggle but rather the steadfastness of spirit in the face of adversity. Trust in your own inner strength and know that you are capable of achieving greatness.

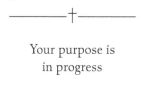

Your purpose is in progress

Your purpose is in progress, as you are on God's path for your life. Regardless of what you face from day to day, remember it is only part of the process and you will make it to the place of promise.

Throughout the Bible, men and women of God endured difficult moments that would make the average person want to give up. Daniel had his experience in the lion's den, Nehemiah had his experience with Sanballot, Tobiah and Gesham, Abraham had his experience with Isaac, Ruth had her experience with Naomi and so many, many more are recorded. Similarly, you have experienced moments that would make others throw in the towel, but not you. You have come too far and there is a great destination that lies ahead of this journey.

We experience difficult moments to further develop our trust and total dependence on Almighty God. There are moments that may be easy for you, and other times that you must purposely push through to experience the greater opportunities that lie ahead.

You have committed to 21 days of prayer, fasting and accountability. Along this journey, there are times that you may feel overwhelmed or fatigued. Yet, you cannot give up or give in because you are destined for a high calling and intense blessing. Stay strong!

Similarly to King David in 1 Samuel 30, you must encourage yourself in the Lord. Remember that the experiences you have now cannot compare to the glory that God is revealing through you. Someone will be blessed by your persistence and perseverance as you await the promise and fulfillment of your purpose.

After this season of 21 days, there will be high moments of triumph and also moments of disappointments, trials, difficulties and hurtful experiences but you must persevere. You must go *through* in order to get *to* the place God wants you to be. You will overcome. You will excel.

You will experience divine intervention and personal transformation. Keep pressing forward–Greater is coming!

May you be blessed with the courage to persevere, the wisdom to navigate life's challenges, and the faith to believe in yourself, now and always. Amen.

PERSONAL TRANSFORMATION ASSIGNMENT

1. What motivates and encourages you?

   _____

   _____

2. How do you renew your strength?

   _____

   _____

3. Sally is a thirty-four year old mother that feels all alone in life. She wants to commit suicide because life has become too difficult for her, and she has been suffering in silence each day. Sally attends church regularly, but recently learned about gossip in the church and does not want to participate any further in activities or festivities. She wants to give up everything. Write words of advice and encouragement that you would give to Sally.

   _____

   _____

4. What similarities do you have with Sally?

   _____

   _____

5. Name a moment in your life that was difficult to endure. How did you make it through?

   _____

   _____

6. Write three quotes, scriptures or popular sayings that will encourage you when you feel overwhelmed on the journey.

_____

_____

_____

7. What part of this journey (Days 1-9) has been easiest for you? Why?

_____

_____

8. What part of this journey (Days 1-9) has been the most difficult for you? Why?

_____

_____

9. Who do you look up to for their fortitude and strength? Why?

_____

_____

10. What three things will be a part of your legacy?

_____

_____

11. Share your testimony from #5 with someone today. Write their name _____

12. Make an effort to encourage three people today. You can send them an email, text, flowers, card or whatever the Lord lays on your heart. Write the names of the people here.

_____

_____

PRAYER

Lord, please renew my strength, restore my joy and remember your promise, in the name of Jesus. Amen.

JOURNAL ENTRY

(Please use this space or your own book designated for this time.)

Today I feel

_____
_____
_____
_____

Lord, I am grateful for

_____
_____
_____
_____

In my life, I look forward to

_____
_____
_____
_____

Today, I have been transformed by

_____
_____
_____
_____

"Regarding other people, our problem is that we need them
(for ourselves) more than we love them (for the glory of God).
The task God sets for us is to need them less and love them more.
Instead of looking for ways to manipulate others,
we will ask God what our duty is toward them."

—Edward T. Welch, <u>When People Are Big and God Is Small:
Overcoming Peer Pressure, Codependency, and the Fear of Man</u>

Day Ten

Word for the day: **PLEASING GOD**

Dear Journey Partner,

The Lord has blessed us bountifully on this journey and we are headed to become wiser, stronger and more determined children of God.

Each day of this 21-Day journey of personal transformation is helping us to develop a closer relationship with the Lord as well as blessing us to further the visions, dreams and goals set out in God's plan and purpose for our lives.

We want to stay at this place of elevation, so we must make sure our lives and Christian walk are pleasing to the Lord.

Today, let us evaluate ourselves and ensure that our relationship with the Lord is our first priority in life.

Greater is coming!

Pastor D

BIBLICAL PASSAGES

Memory Verse: "When a man's ways please the LORD, he makes even his enemies to be at peace with him" (Proverbs 16:7).

"For the Kingdom of God is not a matter of what we eat or drink, but of living a life of goodness and peace and joy in the Holy Spirit. If you serve Christ with this attitude, you will please God. And other people will approve of you, too. So then, let us aim for harmony in the church and try to build each other up" (Romans 14:17-19 NLT).

"I urge you, first of all, to pray for all people. As you make your requests, plead for God's mercy upon them, and give thanks. Pray this way for kings and all others who are in authority, so that we can live in peace and quietness, in godliness and dignity. This is good and pleases God our Savior, for he wants everyone to be saved and to understand the truth. For there is only one God and one Mediator who can reconcile God and people. He is the man Christ Jesus. He gave his life to purchase freedom for everyone. This is the message that God gave to the world at the proper time. And I have been chosen — this is the absolute truth — as a preacher and apostle to teach the Gentiles about faith and truth. So wherever you assemble, I want men to pray with holy hands lifted up to God, free from anger and controversy. And I want women to be modest in their appearance. They should wear decent and appropriate clothing and not draw attention to themselves by the way they fix their hair or by wearing gold or pearls or expensive clothes. For women who claim to be devoted to God should make themselves attractive by the good things they do" (1 Timothy 2:1-10)."This letter is from Paul, chosen by God to be an apostle of Christ Jesus, and from our brother Timothy. It is written to God's holy people in the city of Colossae, who are faithful brothers and sisters in Christ. May God our Father give you grace and peace. We always pray for you, and we give thanks to God the Father of our Lord Jesus Christ, for we have heard that you trust in Christ Jesus and that you love all of God's people. You do this because you are looking forward to the joys of heaven — as you have been ever since you first heard the truth of the Good News. This same Good News that came to you is going out all over the world. It is changing lives everywhere, just as it changed yours that very first day you heard and understood the truth about God's great kindness to sinners. Epaphras, our much loved co-worker, was the one who brought you the Good News. He is Christ's faithful servant, and he is helping us in your place. He is the one who told us about the great love for others that the Holy Spirit has given you. So we have continued praying for you ever since we first heard about you. We ask God to give you a complete understanding of what he wants to do in your lives, and we ask him to make you wise with spiritual wisdom. Then the way you live will always honor and please the Lord, and you will continually do good, kind things for others. All the while, you will learn to know God better and better. We also pray that you will be strengthened with his glorious power so that you will have all the patience and endurance you need. May you be filled with joy, always thanking the Father, who has enabled you to share the inheritance that belongs to God's holy people, who live in the light. For he has rescued us from the one who rules in the kingdom of darkness, and he has brought us into the Kingdom of his dear Son. God has purchased our freedom with his blood and has forgiven all our sins. Christ is the visible image of the invisible God. He existed before God made anything at all and is supreme over all creation. Christ is the one through whom God created everything in heaven and earth. He made the things we can see and the things we can't see — kings, kingdoms, rulers, and authorities. Everything has been created through him and for him. He existed before everything else began, and he holds all creation together. Christ is the head of the church, which is his body. He is the first of all who will rise from the dead, so he is first in everything. For God in all his fullness was pleased to live in Christ, and by him God reconciled everything to himself. He made peace with everything in heaven and on earth by means of his blood on the cross. This includes you who were once so far away from

God. You were his enemies, separated from him by your evil thoughts and actions, yet now he has brought you back as his friends. He has done this through his death on the cross in his own human body. As a result, he has brought you into the very presence of God, and you are holy and blameless as you stand before him without a single fault. But you must continue to believe this truth and stand in it firmly. Don't drift away from the assurance you received when you heard the Good News. The Good News has been preached all over the world, and I, Paul, have been appointed by God to proclaim it. I am glad when I suffer for you in my body, for I am completing what remains of Christ's sufferings for his body, the church" (Colossians 1:1-24).

PERSONAL ASSESSMENT

1. Is your life pleasing to God? Why or Why not?

_____

_____

2. What things in your past were not pleasing to God?

_____

_____

3. What are you doing to ensure you will not repeat the past mistakes?

_____

_____

4. What things are you doing presently that are pleasing to God?

_____

_____

5. How do you feel at this stage of the journey?

_____

_____

LIFE TRANSFORMATION MESSAGE

My friend, we spend a great amount of time trying to please ourselves and others. We are constantly trying to make others happy and bless their lives. Yet, it is not the opinions of others that will determine our destiny; it is the call of God. The Lord is calling you and me to a higher place of blessing as well as a higher place of accountability. Our ways must please the Lord.

Today, please read the biblical passages and centralize your focus on living a life that is pleasing to God. There are miraculous blessings that will be released in our lives when our thoughts, attitudes, behaviors and actions please God. Above everything, make sure you are living right and serving with a heart of love.

Remember, you are simply a traveler on Earth and your ultimate destination is Heaven. Do NOT allow anyone or anything to pull you off course from your divine assignment and place of destiny. Instead, focus on a right relationship with the Lord and trust God to perfect all things that concern you.

In Galatians 1:10, The Apostle Paul writes, "For am I now seeking the approval of man, or of God? Or am I trying to please man? If I were still trying to please man, I would not be a servant of Christ." This verse reminds us that our primary allegiance is to God, not to the opinions or approval of others.

Furthermore, in Matthew 6:1, Jesus warns against practicing our righteousness before others in order to be seen by them. He encourages us to seek God's approval rather than the applause of the crowd. When we prioritize pleasing God, our actions are guided by love, integrity, and obedience to His Word.

Living to please God means aligning our thoughts, words, and deeds with His will. As it says in Colossians 3:23, "Whatever you do, work heartily, as for the Lord and not for men." Whether it's in our relationships, our work, or our daily interactions, our aim should be to honor God above all else.

When we seek the approval of people, we can fall into the trap of compromise and hypocrisy. However, when our focus is on pleasing God, we find freedom from the burden of trying to measure up to others' expectations. Instead, we find joy and fulfillment in knowing that our lives are pleasing to the One who matters most.

———†———

> When our focus is on pleasing God, we find freedom from the burden of trying to measure up to others' expectations.

Let us remember the words of Romans 12:2: "Do not be conformed to this world, but be transformed by the renewal of your mind, that by testing you may discern what is the will of God, what is good and acceptable and perfect." As we renew our minds and live according to God's will, we will experience the true abundance and satisfaction that comes from pleasing God.

May we all strive to live lives that bring glory and honor to God, seeking His approval above all else. Amen.

PERSONAL TRANSFORMATION ASSIGNMENT

1. Read 1 Thessalonians 2:1-4. Write down your interpretation of this scripture and how it applies to your life presently.

   _____

   _____

2. What three things did you learn from today's biblical passage?

   _____

   _____

3. Study Asa in 1 Chronicles 14:2. How was Asa pleasing to God? What can we glean from Asa's life?

   _____

   _____

4. Name a moment in your life that you are proud of when you recall it.

   _____

   _____

5. How do you believe God views you and your current state of being? Why?

   _____

   _____

6. What part of this lesson has provoked the most thought? Why?

   _____

   _____

7. What part of this journey is compelling you to action in your personal walk with God? How?

_____

_____

8. Journal at least five changes you have made in your life recently.

_____

_____

9. Who has made a lasting impact on your life? How?

_____

_____

10. Write an acronym below for Pleasing God–P L E A S E

    P _____

    L _____

    E _____

    A _____

    S _____

    E _____

PRAYER

Lord, let the words of mouth, the meditations of my heart and the actions in my life be pleasing in your sight. Amen.

JOURNAL ENTRY

(Please use this space or your own book designated for this time.)

Lord, please forgive me for

_____

_____

_____

_____

Lord, I want to please you by

_____

_____

_____

_____

In my life, I want to be remembered for

_____

_____

_____

_____

Today, I have been transformed by

_____

_____

_____

_____

"Thanksgiving is inseparable from true prayer; it is almost essentially connected with it. One who always prays is ever giving praise, whether in ease or pain, both for prosperity and for the greatest adversity. He blesses God for all things, looks on them as coming from Him, and receives them for His sake- not choosing nor refusing, liking or disliking, anything, but only as it is agreeable or disagreeable to His perfect will."

—**John Wesley, <u>How to Pray: The Best of John Wesley on Prayer</u>**

Day Eleven

~~~~~~

Word for the day: **PRAISE**

Dear Journey Partner,

This has been an engaging, thought provoking time of personal transformation. We are reminded that everything we have experienced and all that will come to pass in our lives is because of God's love and grace in our lives.

God does not require as much from us as we have been given. The main thing God created mankind to do is praise God. A part of our daily plan should be time carved just to honor God for the bountiful blessings in our lives and this spectacular universe in which we live.

God has been so good to us, and has an amazing plan for your future. Today, we pause to praise God with our whole hearts. Glory, honor and majesty belong to our God!

Set aside time today and everyday to praise the God who loved you before you were shaped, and will continue to be with you throughout eternity.

Greater is coming!

Pastor D

BIBLICAL PASSAGES

Memory Verse: "When a man's ways please the LORD, he makes even his enemies to be at peace with him" (Proverbs 16:7).

"For the Kingdom of God is not a matter of what we eat or drink, but of living a life of goodness and peace and joy in the Holy Spirit. If you serve Christ with this attitude, you will please God. And other people will approve of you, too. So then, let us aim for harmony in the church and try to build each other up" (Romans 14:17-19 NLT).

"I urge you, first of all, to pray for all people. As you make your requests, plead for God's mercy upon them, and give thanks. Pray this way for kings and all others who are in authority, so that we can live in peace and quietness, in godliness and dignity. This is good and pleases God our Savior, for he wants everyone to be saved and to understand the truth. For there is only one God and one Mediator who can reconcile God and people. He is the man Christ Jesus. He gave his life to purchase freedom for everyone. This is the message that God gave to the world at the proper time. And I have been chosen — this is the absolute truth — as a preacher and apostle to teach the Gentiles about faith and truth. So wherever you assemble, I want men to pray with holy hands lifted up to God, free from anger and controversy. And I want women to be modest in their appearance. They should wear decent and appropriate clothing and not draw attention to themselves by the way they fix their hair or by wearing gold or pearls or expensive clothes. For women who claim to be devoted to God should make themselves attractive by the good things they do" (1 Timothy 2:1-10).

"This letter is from Paul, chosen by God to be an apostle of Christ Jesus, and from our brother Timothy. It is written to God's holy people in the city of Colossae, who are faithful brothers and sisters in Christ. May God our Father give you grace and peace. We always pray for you, and we give thanks to God the Father of our Lord Jesus Christ, for we have heard that you trust in Christ Jesus and that you love all of God's people. You do this because you are looking forward to the joys of heaven — as you have been ever since you first heard the truth of the Good News. This same Good News that came to you is going out all over the world. It is changing lives everywhere, just as it changed yours that very first day you heard and understood the truth about God's great kindness to sinners. Epaphras, our much loved co-worker, was the one who brought you the Good News. He is Christ's faithful servant, and he is helping us in your place. He is the one who told us about the great love for others that the Holy Spirit has given you. So we have continued praying for you ever since we first heard about you. We ask God to give you a complete understanding of what he wants to do in your lives, and we ask him to make you wise with spiritual wisdom. Then the way you live will always honor and please the Lord, and you will continually do good, kind things for others. All the while, you will learn to know God better and better. We also pray that you will be strengthened with his glorious power so that you will have all the patience and endurance you need. May you be filled with joy, always thanking the Father, who has enabled you to share the inheritance that belongs to God's holy people, who live in the light. For he has rescued us from the one who rules in the kingdom of darkness, and he has brought us into the Kingdom of his dear Son. God has purchased our freedom with his blood and has forgiven all our sins. Christ is the visible image of the invisible God. He existed before God made anything at all and is supreme over all creation. Christ is the one through whom God created everything in heaven and earth. He made the things we can see and the things we can't see — kings, kingdoms, rulers, and authorities. Everything has been created through him and for him. He existed before everything else began, and he holds all creation together. Christ is the head of the church, which is his body. He is the first of all who will rise from the dead, so he is first in everything. For God in all his fullness was pleased to live in Christ, and by him God reconciled everything to himself. He made peace with everything in heaven and on earth by means of his blood on the cross. This includes you who were once so far away from God. You were his enemies, separated from him by your evil thoughts and actions, yet now he has brought you back as his friends. He has done this through his death on the cross in his own human body. As a result, he has brought you into the very presence of God, and you are holy and blameless as you stand before him without a single fault. But you must continue to believe this truth and stand in it firmly. Don't drift away from the assurance you received when you heard the Good News. The Good News has been preached all over the world, and I, Paul, have been appointed by God to proclaim it. I am glad when I suffer for you in my body, for I am completing what remains of Christ's sufferings for his body, the church" (Colossians 1:1-24).

PERSONAL ASSESSMENT

1. What is praise?

   _____

   _____

2. How do you praise?

   _____

   _____

3. Who do you praise?

   _____

   _____

4. When do you praise?

   _____

   _____

5. What does praise do for your spirit?

   _____

   _____

6. How does praise affect your relationship with God? What does praise do for your spirit?

   _____

   _____

7. Do you fulfill the commandment on praise? Why or why not?

   _____

   _____

LIFE TRANSFORMATION MESSAGE

Our hearts are lifted in adoration when we reflect on the majesty, goodness, and faithfulness of God. In Psalm 150:6, we are reminded, "Let everything that has breath praise God!" Our very existence is a testament to the greatness of our Creator, and praising God is our natural response to God's love and grace.

> When we make praise a constant practice in our lives, we cultivate a deep intimacy with God and align ourselves with divine purposes.

Praising God is not merely an expectation of a Christian believer, but a privilege. It opens our hearts to God's presence and fills us with God's peace and joy. In Psalm 34:1, we read, "I will bless God at all times; His praise shall continually be in my mouth." When we make praise a constant practice in our lives, we cultivate a deep intimacy with God and align ourselves with divine purposes.

Moreover, praising God shifts our focus from ourselves to the One who deserves all honor and glory. In Psalm 145:3, we are reminded, "Great is God, and greatly to be praised, and God's greatness is unsearchable." When we magnify God in our lives, we acknowledge God's sovereignty and power over every circumstance, finding strength and hope in God's presence.

Living a life of praise transforms us from the inside out. It fills us with gratitude and humility, grounding us in the reality of God's love and provision. In Hebrews 13:15, we are urged, "Through Jesus, therefore, let us continually offer to God a sacrifice of praise—the fruit of lips that openly profess God's name." Our praise becomes a sacred offering, a testament to our faith and devotion.

Let us embrace the call to live lives of praise, not just in moments of joy or abundance but in every season and circumstance. For in praising God, we align ourselves with the rhythm of God's love and grace and find our truest fulfillment in God's presence. May our lives resound with the melody of praise, bringing glory and honor to God, now and forevermore. Amen.

PERSONAL TRANSFORMATION ASSIGNMENT

1. Write 100 things you praise God for today.

   _____

   _____

   _____

   _____

   _____

   _____

   _____

   _____

   _____

   _____

   _____

2. Read through each of the experiences from aboveand recite "Lord, I praise you for _____. Hallelujah! Praise your name." Take your time and express love and appreciation to the Lord.

   _____

   _____

3. Name three experiences of your past that has allowed you to grow in wisdom and understanding.

   _____

   _____

4. Record a testimony of a miracle in your life.

   _____

   _____

5. Who is God to you? (example: deliverer)

_____

_____

6. What things do you believe God will do for you this year?

_____

_____

7. Write a poem or song of personal praise.

_____

_____

_____

_____

_____

PRAYER

Lord, let the words of mouth, the meditations of my heart and the actions in my life be pleasing in your sight. Amen.

JOURNAL ENTRY

(Please use this space or your own book designated for this time.)

Today, I feel

_____

_____

_____

_____

My life has been

_____

_____

_____

_____

The Lord has shown me love by

_____

_____

_____

_____

Today, I have been transformed by

_____

_____

_____

_____

"Each of us must decide whether it is more important to be proved right or to provoke righteousness."

Rev. Bernice King

Day Twelve

<><><><><><><><><><><><><><><><><><><><><><><><><><><><><><><><><><><><><><><><><><><><>

Word for the day: **PURSUIT OF RIGHTEOUSNESS**

Dear Journey Partner,

Our focus for today is the pursuit of righteousness. More than anything, we should seek to be like the Lord. There are blessings in store for those who want to be like Jesus. This doesn't call for perfection, but instead, someone with a transformed heart to love and bless others. Today, let's evaluate our lifestyles and continue in the path for life transformation. You are shifting for a major upgrade in life.

Greater is coming!

Pastor D

BIBLICAL PASSAGES

Memory Verse: "Blessed are they which do hunger and thirst after righteousness, for they shall be filled" (Matthew 5:6).

"The king's heart is like a stream of water directed by the LORD; he turns it wherever he pleases. People may think they are doing what is right, but the LORD examines the heart. The LORD is more pleased when we do what is just and right than when we give him sacrifices. Haughty eyes, a proud heart, and evil actions are all sin. Good planning and hard work lead to prosperity, but hasty shortcuts lead to poverty. Wealth created by lying is a vanishing mist and a deadly trap. Because the wicked refuse to do what is just, their violence boomerangs and destroys them. The guilty walk a crooked path; the innocent travel a straight road. It is better to live alone in the corner of an attic than with a contentious wife in a lovely home. Evil people love to harm others; their neighbors get no mercy from them. A simpleton can learn only by seeing mockers punished; a wise person learns from instruction. The Righteous One knows what is going on in the homes of the wicked; he will bring the wicked to disaster. Those who shut their ears to the cries of the poor will be ignored in their own time of need. A secret gift calms anger; a secret bribe pacifies fury. Justice is a joy to the godly, but it causes dismay among evildoers. The person who strays from common sense will end up in the company of the dead. Those who love pleasure become poor; wine and luxury are not the way to riches. Sometimes the wicked are punished to save the godly, and the treacherous for the upright. It is better to live alone in the desert than with a crabby, complaining wife. The wise have wealth and luxury, but fools spend whatever they get. Whoever pursues godliness and unfailing love will find life, godliness, and honor. The wise conquer the city of the strong and level the fortress in which they trust. If you keep your mouth shut, you will stay out of trouble. Mockers are proud and haughty; they act with boundless arrogance. The desires of lazy people will be their ruin, for their hands refuse to work. They are always greedy for more, while the godly love to give! God loathes the sacrifice of an evil person, especially when it is brought with ulterior motives. A false witness will be cut off, but an attentive witness will be allowed to speak. The wicked put up a bold front, but the upright proceed with care. Human plans, no matter how wise or well advised, cannot stand against the LORD. The horses are prepared for battle, but the victory belongs to the LORD" (Proverbs 21).

"For we know that when this earthly tent we live in is taken down — when we die and leave these bodies — we will have a home in heaven, an eternal body made for us by God himself and not by human hands. We grow weary in our present bodies, and we long for the day when we will put on our heavenly bodies like new clothing. For we will not be spirits without bodies, but we will put on new heavenly bodies. Our dying bodies make us groan and sigh, but it's not that we want to die and have no bodies at all. We want to slip into our new bodies so that these dying bodies will be swallowed up by everlasting life. God himself has prepared us for this, and as a guarantee he has given us his Holy Spirit. So we are always confident, even though we know that as long as we live in these bodies we are not at home with the Lord. That is why we live by believing and not by seeing. Yes, we are fully confident, and we would rather be away from these bodies, for then we will be at home with the Lord. So our aim is to please him always, whether we are here in this body or away from this body. For we must all stand before Christ to be judged. We will each receive whatever we deserve for the good or evil we have done in our bodies. It is because we know this solemn fear of the Lord that we work so hard to persuade others. God knows we are sincere, and I hope you know this, too. Are we trying to pat ourselves on the back again? No, we are giving you a reason to be proud of us, so you can answer those who brag about having a spectacular ministry rather than having a sincere heart before God. If it seems that we are crazy, it is to bring glory to God. And if we are in our right minds, it is for your benefit. Whatever we do, it is because Christ's love controls us. Since we believe that Christ died for everyone, we also believe that we have all died to the old life we used to live. He died for everyone so that those who receive his new life will no longer live to please themselves. Instead, they will live to please Christ, who died and was raised for them. So we have stopped evaluating others by what the world thinks about them. Once I mistakenly thought of Christ that way, as though he were merely a human being. How differently I think about him now! What this means is that those who become Christians become new persons. They are not the same anymore, for the old life is gone. A new life has begun! All this newness of life is from God, who brought us back to himself through what Christ did. And God has given us the task of reconciling people to him. For God was in Christ, reconciling the world to himself, no longer counting people's sins against them. This is the wonderful message he has given us to tell others. We are Christ's ambassadors, and God is using us to speak to you. We urge you, as though Christ himself were here pleading with you, "Be reconciled to God!" For God made Christ, who never sinned, to be the offering for our sin, so that we could be made right with God through Christ" (2 Corinthian 5).

PERSONAL ASSESSMENT

1. What is righteousness?

   _____

   _____

2. Are you righteous before God?

   _____

   _____

3. What part of your life is not righteous and holy before the Lord?

   _____

   _____

4. What are the main things of importance in your life?

   _____

   _____

5. Describe yourself in one statement

   _____

   _____

LIFE TRANSFORMATION MESSAGE

Today, let us reflect on the profound importance of striving for righteousness in our lives. Righteousness is not merely a set of rules to follow but a way of living in alignment with God's truth and holiness. In Matthew 6:33, Jesus instructs us, "But seek first his kingdom and his righteousness, and all these things will be given to you as well." When we prioritize righteousness, we align ourselves with God's will and open ourselves to His abundant blessings.

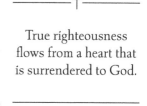

When we prioritize righteousness, we align ourselves with God's will and open ourselves to His abundant blessings.

Striving for righteousness is a continuous journey of growth and transformation. It requires a commitment to integrity, honesty, and justice in all areas of our lives. As recorded in Proverbs 11:3, "The integrity of the upright guides them, but the unfaithful are destroyed by their duplicity." When we walk in righteousness, we experience inner peace and fulfillment, knowing that our lives are pleasing to God.

Moreover, righteousness is not just about our actions but also about the condition of our hearts. In Matthew 5:20, Jesus declares, "For I tell you, unless your righteousness exceeds that of the scribes and Pharisees, you will never enter the kingdom of heaven." True righteousness flows from a heart that is surrendered to God, filled with love, compassion, and humility.

True righteousness flows from a heart that is surrendered to God.

Living a life of righteousness sets us apart as lights in a dark world. In Ephesians 5:8, we are reminded, "For you were once darkness, but now you are light in the Lord. Live as children of light." Our commitment to righteousness shines as a beacon of hope and truth, drawing others to God's love and grace.

The way you live has a direct impact on your relationship with Almighty God and the image before others. Righteousness is a state we should strive for each day. The Beatitudes reminds us that we must hunger and thirst for righteousness and we will be filled.

God does not expect us to be perfect, but God does expect us to strive for perfection. Do not give in easily or make excuses for wrong behavior, attitudes and ways.

————†————

God does not expect us to be perfect, but God does expect us to strive for perfection.

We have outlined serious and ambitious goals, dreams and visions for this new season of our lives. In order to attain these things, we must focus on being in right relationship with God and others.

As you read the scriptures for today and apply them to your life, remember that God honors those whose hearts are pure and focused on God's will. Our future is bigger than a new house, car or money – we are leaving a legacy for those who will come behind us in life. Let us ensure that our life and our works speak well of us.

This is not a day for accolades, but it is a time of accommodation and adjustment. The results will be rewarding for days, months and years to come. Keep your heart and mind focused on the Lord and God's ultimate plan and purpose for you.

Striving for righteousness is not always easy and we may face challenges and temptations along the way. Nevertheless, as recorded in 1 Timothy 6:11, "But you, man of God, flee from all this, and pursue righteousness, godliness, faith, love, endurance and gentleness." Let us press on, knowing that our efforts are not in vain and that God rewards those who diligently seek Him.

May we all be inspired to strive for righteousness in our lives, knowing that in doing so, we bring glory and honor to our Heavenly Creator. Let us walk in the footsteps of Jesus, our ultimate example of righteousness, and may God's grace empower us to live lives that reflect unconditional love and truth to the world. Amen.

PERSONAL TRANSFORMATION ASSIGNMENT

1. Read James 5:16 and write your interpretation of this scripture.

    _____

    _____

2. What does James 3:18 mean at this stage of your life?

    _____

    _____

3. Name a biblical character that was righteous before the Lord. Name the characteristics of this person that you would like in your life.

    _____

    _____

4. Name a person you have come in contact with that appeared to be righteous.

    _____

    _____

5. When was the last time you were in right relationship with God?

    _____

    _____

6. What is the penalty for anyone that is not righteous?

    _____

    _____

7. What has been the most thought-provoking part of this lesson?

    _____

    _____

8. Write a quote or poem about righteousness.

   _____

   _____

9. Name three ways you can apply today's lesson to your life.

   _____

   _____

10. Using the following chart, please write rate the number of importance for each part of your life. (1-15) 1 = most important, 15 = least important_____

    _____

Family	
My relationship with God	
Job	
Money	
Marriage	
My testimony	
Friendship	
Possessions	
Reputation	
Future Plans	
Church	
Community	
Health	
Politics	
Spiritual Gifts	

PRAYER

Dear Lord, I surrender my will and I seek to be more like you, in the name of Jesus. Amen.

JOURNAL ENTRY

(Please use this space or your own book designated for this time.)

Righteousness is

_____

_____

_____

_____

I am proud of myself for

_____

_____

_____

_____

I believe God thinks of me as

_____

_____

_____

_____

Today, I have been transformed by

_____

_____

_____

_____

"There is nothing noble in being superior to your fellow man; true nobility is being superior to your former self."

—Ernest Hemingway

Day Thirteen

Word for the day: **PRIDE**

Dear Journey Partner,

Our focus for today is pride. We must be careful in our journey experiences that we remain humble and personable and not allow arrogance and pride to be our character attributes. We should think well of ourselves and be confident in our abilities, but above that – we should always be mindful of the grace and mercy that prevails in our lives.

During this season, we must strip the things that are not like the Lord, so they will not serve as a hindrance in the realization of dreams and goals. God is not only doing a new thing in you; God is creating a new you!

Let go and let God. The results will ensure that many are blessed by your experience and testimony.

Greater is coming!

Pastor D

BIBLICAL PASSAGES

Memory Verse: "Pride goes before destruction, and haughtiness before a fall" (Proverbs 16:18 NLT).

"In Jerusalem he [King Uzziah] made machines, invented by skillful men, to be on the towers and the corners, to shoot arrows and great stones. And his fame spread far, for he was marvelously helped, till he was strong. But when he was strong, he grew proud, to his destruction. For he was unfaithful to the Lord his God and entered the temple of the Lord to burn incense on the altar of incense." (2 Chronicles 26:15-16)

"For the wicked boasts of the desires of his soul, and the one greedy for gain curses and renounces the Lord. In the pride of his face the wicked does not seek him; all his thoughts are, 'There is no God.'" (Psalms 10:3-4)

"For the sin of their mouths, the words of their lips, let them be trapped in their pride." (Psalm 59:12)

There are six things that the Lord hates, seven that are an abomination to him: haughty eyes, a lying tongue, and hands that shed innocent blood, a heart that devises wicked plans, feet that make haste to run to evil, a false witness who breathes out lies, and one who sows discord among brothers." (Proverbs 6:16-19)

"The fear of the Lord is hatred of evil. Pride and arrogance and the way of evil and perverted speech I hate." (Proverbs 8:13)

"How you are fallen from heaven, O Day Star, son of Dawn! How you are cut down to the ground, you who laid the nations low! You said in your heart, 'I will ascend to heaven; above the stars of God I will set my throne on high; I will sit on the mount of assembly in the far reaches of the north; I will ascend above the heights of the clouds; I will make myself like the Most High.'" (Isaiah 14:12-14)

"Again, the devil took him to a very high mountain and showed him all the kingdoms of the world and their glory. And he said to him, 'All these I will give you, if you will fall down and worship me.'" (Matthew 4:8-9)

"But Hezekiah did not make return according to the benefit done to him, for his heart was proud. Therefore wrath came upon him and Judah and Jerusalem. But Hezekiah humbled himself for the pride of his heart, both he and the inhabitants of Jerusalem, so that the wrath of the Lord did not come upon them in the days of Hezekiah." (2 Chronicles 32:25-26)

"When the Lord has finished all his work on Mount Zion and on Jerusalem, he will punish the speech of the arrogant heart of the king of Assyria and the boastful look in his eyes." (Isaiah 10:12)

"He also told this parable to some who trusted in themselves that they were righteous, and treated others with contempt: 'Two men went up into the temple to pray, one a Pharisee and the other a tax collector. The Pharisee, standing by himself, prayed thus: 'God, I thank you that I am not like other men, extortioners, unjust, adulterers, or even like this tax collector. I fast twice a week; I give tithes of all that I get.' But the tax collector, standing far off, would not even lift up his eyes to heaven, but beat his breast, saying, 'God, be merciful to me, a sinner!' I tell you, this man went down to his house justified, rather than the other. For everyone who exalts himself will be humbled, but the one who humbles himself will be exalted.'" (Luke 18:9-14)

"On an appointed day Herod put on his royal robes, took his seat upon the throne, and delivered an oration to them. And the people were shouting, 'The voice of a god, and not of a man!' Immediately an angel of the Lord struck him down, because he did not give God the glory, and he was eaten by worms and breathed his last." (Acts 12:21-23)

"And if in spite of this you will not listen to me, then I will discipline you again sevenfold for your sins, and I will break the pride of your power, and I will make your heavens like iron and your earth like bronze. And your strength shall be spent in vain, for your land shall not yield its increase, and the trees of the land shall not yield their fruit." (Leviticus 26:18-20)

"The Lord said: Because the daughters of Zion are haughty and walk with outstretched necks, glancing wantonly with their eyes, mincing along as they go, tinkling with their feet, therefore the Lord will strike with a scab the heads of the daughters of Zion, and the Lord will lay bare their secret parts." (Isaiah 3:16-17)

"On that day you shall not be put to shame because of the deeds by which you have rebelled against me; for then I will remove from your midst your proudly exultant ones, and you shall no longer be haughty in my holy mountain." (Zephaniah 3:11)

PERSONAL ASSESSMENT

1. What is pride?
   _____
   _____

2. Is there any evidence of pride in your life?
   _____
   _____

3. Who do you rely upon?
   _____
   _____

4. Name your five most significant character attributes.
   _____
   _____

5. How do you feel today?
   _____
   _____

LIFE TRANSFORMATION MESSAGE

As we upgrade our lives, we must reflect on the virtue of humility and the importance of removing pride from our lives. Pride, though often disguised as confidence or self-assurance, can be a stumbling block on our spiritual journey, hindering our growth and distancing us from the grace of God.

In a world that often celebrates individual achievement and self-promotion, it can be all too easy to succumb to the allure of pride. We may become consumed by our own accomplishments, seeking recognition and validation from others, and forgetting the source of all true blessings.

But let us be reminded, my dear brothers and sisters, that true greatness lies not in the exaltation of self but in the humble service of others. Jesus Himself exemplified this principle, by washing the feet of His disciples and teaching us that the path to greatness is found in the posture of a servant.

> The path to greatness is found in the posture of a servant.

In order to reach a high plateau in your walk with the Lord this year, it is essential to evaluate your personality and characteristics that may obstruct your path or mislead someone else. Pride is a character trait that can make us seem rude, arrogant, ungrateful, and intolerable. We may not mean to appear this way at all, but sometimes confidence is driven by human attributes and clouds our true hearts and intentions.

As we upgrade our lives, we must continually evaluate ourselves – personalities, goals, inner circle – and ensure we are seeking a transformation of our entire being. God is not only taking your visions and dreams to the next level; God is taking you higher! You must become a better person. That will involve the foundation of your relationship with Him and a continued search for faithfulness and dedication. You must change, so God can use you in a more magnificent way.

Greater is coming. Therefore, we must remove the guilt, pain, ignorance, arrogance, hatred, bitterness, and inconsistencies in our lives to make room for the prosperity, peace, power, position and purity that will come as a replacement.

Today, read the biblical passages and meditate on the word of God. Ask God to show you ways you have exhibited the spirit of pride and cleanse yourself from those ways. Evaluate who you are and make a conscious decision to live better than you have in the past. Remember, "To whom much is given, much is required."

You are on your way to a new level and assignment. This lesson will allow you to shed some ways and attributes, as you focus on what is most important for the future. It's your time and season for grace, favor and humility.

Humility is not a sign of weakness but rather, a mark of strength. It requires us to acknowledge our own limitations and imperfections and to recognize the inherent worth and dignity of every human being. It is through humility that we open ourselves to the transformative power of God's love and grace.

> It is through humility that we open ourselves to the transformative power of God's love and grace.

Let us also remember that pride often leads to division and conflict, as we become more concerned with proving ourselves right than with seeking understanding and reconciliation. By cultivating humility in our hearts, we create space for empathy, compassion, and unity to flourish.

So, friends, let us strive to remove pride from our lives and to walk humbly in the footsteps of our Lord. Let us seek not the praise of others, but the approval of God, who sees into the depths of our souls and calls us to lives of righteousness and compassion.

May we be inspired by the words of the Apostle Paul, who reminds us to "Do nothing out of selfish ambition or vain conceit. Rather, in humility value others above yourselves, not looking to your own interests but each of you to the interests of the others." (Philippians 2:3)

May we, too, embody this spirit of humility in all that we do, and may it lead us ever closer to the heart of God. Amen.

PERSONAL TRANSFORMATION ASSIGNMENT

1. Read Job 20:6 and write your interpretation of this scripture.

    _____

    _____

2. What does Proverbs 11:2 mean to you at this stage of your life?

    _____

    _____

3. Name a biblical character that exhibited pride or arrogance. Name other outstanding characteristics of this person.

    _____

    _____

4. Name a person you have come in contact with that had great pride. Do you remember that time in a positive way or a negative way? Why?

    _____

    _____

5. Name a time in your life that you responded with pride.

    _____

    _____

6. Have you ever been punished for your pride?

    _____

    _____

7. What has been the most thought-provoking part of this lesson?

_____

_____

8. What advice would you give to an arrogant person that wants to change?

_____

_____

9. Name three ways you can apply today's lesson to your life.

_____

_____

10. Write five ways to remove the spirit of pride from a person's life.

_____

_____

11. Enact those five ways from #10 in your life over the next 72 hours.

_____

_____

12. Communicate with a person that has known you for ten years or more and will be objective and truthful in conversation. Ask them specifically, "Do you think I am arrogant?" and write down their response. Do not try to change their mind or argue a point with them. God will give you discernment on how to process the statement.

_____

_____

13. Spend time in prayer, asking God to forgive you for any way you have operated in pride and to deliver you from it.

_____

_____

PRAYER

Dear Lord, help me to mirror your image and to be humble in the sight of others, in the name of Jesus, Amen.

JOURNAL ENTRY

(Please use this space or your own book designated for this time.)

Today, I must confess that I am

_____

_____

_____

_____

I must adjust my attitude about pride by

_____

_____

_____

_____

I want to focus on

_____

_____

_____

_____

Today, I have been transformed by

_____

_____

_____

_____

"Prosperity is the divine enablement that helps you overcome obstacles in order to fulfill a purpose—the capacity you need to maximize your potential to create change."

Minister Cindy Trimm, Command Your Morning

Day Fourteen

Word for the day: **PROSPERITY**

Dear Journey Partner,

The Lord is doing a tremendous work in you and the best is yet to come! Yesterday, we attacked a spirit that could hold our blessings hostage and today we are praying the release of mighty miracles in the supernatural. Get ready – you are about to experience abundance and overflow as you trust in the Lord to perfect all that concerns you! Regardless of what it looks like, the Lord will prosper you and take you higher. You will have more than enough to conquer anything and everything you face now and forever.

Greater is coming!

Pastor D

BIBLICAL PASSAGES

Memory Verse: "Good planning and hard work lead to prosperity, but hasty shortcuts lead to poverty" (Proverbs 21:5 NLT).

"I shall not die, but live, And declare the works of the Lord. The Lord has chastened me severely, But He has not given me over to death. Open to me the gates of righteousness; I will go through them, And I will praise the Lord. This is the gate of the Lord, Through which the righteous shall enter. I will praise You, For You have answered me, And have become my salvation. The stone which the builders rejected Has become the chief cornerstone. This was the Lord's doing; It is marvelous in our eyes. This is the day the Lord has made; We will rejoice and be glad in it. Save now, I pray, O Lord; O Lord, I pray, send now prosperity. Blessed is he who comes in the name of the Lord! We have blessed you from the house of the Lord. God is the Lord, And He has given us light; Bind the sacrifice with cords to the horns of the altar. You are my God, and I will praise You; You are my God, I will exalt You. Oh, give thanks to the Lord, for He is good! For His mercy endures forever" (Psalm 118:17-29).

"Moreover the word of the Lord came to Jeremiah a second time, while he was still shut up in the court of the prison, saying, 'Thus says the Lord who made it, the Lord who formed it to establish it (the Lord is His name):Call to Me, and I will answer you, and show you great and mighty things, which you do not know. 'For thus says the Lord, the God of Israel, concerning the houses of this city and the houses of the kings of Judah, which have been pulled down to fortify against the siege mounds and the sword: 'They come to fight with the Chaldeans, but only to fill their places with the dead bodies of men whom I will slay in My anger and My fury, all for whose wickedness I have hidden My face from this city. Behold, I will bring it health and healing; I will heal them and reveal to them the abundance of peace and truth. And I will cause the captives of Judah and the captives of Israel to return, and will rebuild those places as at the first. I will cleanse them from all their iniquity by which they have sinned against Me, and I will pardon all their iniquities by which they have sinned and by which they have transgressed against Me. Then it shall be to Me a name of joy, a praise, and an honor before all nations of the earth, who shall hear all the good that I do to them; they shall fear and tremble for all the goodness and all the prosperity that I provide for it.' Thus says the Lord: 'Again there shall be heard in this place—of which you say, It is desolate, without man and without beast—in the cities of Judah, in the streets of Jerusalem that are desolate, without man and without inhabitant and without beast, the voice of joy and the voice of gladness, the voice of the bridegroom and the voice of the bride, the voice of those who will say: 'Praise the Lord of hosts, For the Lord is good, For His mercy endures forever and of those who will bring the sacrifice of praise into the house of the Lord. For I will cause the captives of the land to return as at the first,' says the Lord. Thus says the Lord of hosts: 'In this place which is desolate, without man and without beast, and in all its cities, there shall again be a dwelling place of shepherds causing their flocks to lie down. In the cities of the mountains, in the cities of the lowland, in the cities of the South, in the land of Benjamin, in the places around Jerusalem, and in the cities of Judah, the flocks shall again pass under the hands of him who counts them,' says the Lord. 'Behold, the days are coming,' says the Lord, 'that I will perform that good thing which I have promised to the house of Israel and to the house of Judah: In those days and at that time I will cause to grow up to David A Branch of righteousness; He shall execute judgment and righteousness in the earth. In those days Judah will be saved, And Jerusalem will dwell safely. And this is the name by which she will be called: THE LORD OUR RIGHTEOUSNESS'" (Jeremiah 33:1-17).

"Behold, God is mighty, but despises no one; He is mighty in strength of understanding. He does not preserve the life of the wicked, But gives justice to the oppressed. He does not withdraw His eyes from the righteous; But they are on the throne with kings, For He has seated them forever, And they are exalted. And if they are bound in fetters, Held in the cords of affliction, Then He tells them their work and their transgressions— That they have acted defiantly. He also opens their ear to instruction, And commands that they turn from iniquity. If they obey and serve Him, They shall spend their days in prosperity, And their years in pleasures. But if they do not obey, They shall perish by the sword, And they shall die without knowledge. But the hypocrites in heart store up wrath; They do not cry for help when He binds them. They die in youth, And their life ends among the perverted persons. He delivers the poor in their affliction, And opens their ears in oppression. Indeed He would have brought you out of dire distress, Into a broad place where there is no restraint; And what is set on your table would be full of richness. But you are filled with the judgment due the wicked; Judgment and justice take hold of you. Because there is wrath, beware lest He take you away with one blow; For a large ransom would not help you avoid it. Will your riches, Or all the mighty forces, Keep you from distress? Do not desire the night, When people are cut off in their place. Take heed, do not turn to iniquity, For you have chosen this rather than affliction" (Job 36:5-21).

"Let them shout for joy and be glad, who favor my righteous cause; And let them say continually, 'Let the Lord be magnified, Who has pleasure in the prosperity of His servant.' And my tongue shall speak of Your righteousness And of Your praise all the day long" (Psalm 35:27-28).

PERSONAL ASSESSMENT

1. What is prosperity?
   _____
   _____

2. Are you prospering spiritually? Why or why not?
   _____
   _____

3. Are you prospering socially? Why or why not?
   _____
   _____

4. Are you prospering economically? Why or why not?
   _____
   _____

5. Are you prospering physically? Why or why not?
   _____
   _____

6. Which area are you doing the best?
   _____
   _____

7. Which area needs the most improvement?
   _____
   _____

LIFE TRANSFORMATION MESSAGE

The abundant blessings of prosperity surround us each day. As children of a loving and generous God, we are called to live lives of prosperity, not only in material wealth but also in spiritual abundance.

Prosperity, in its truest sense, is not merely the accumulation of possessions or the attainment of worldly success. It is a state of being characterized by flourishing in every aspect of our lives – physically, emotionally, financially, and spiritually.

Yet, prosperity is not always easy to attain nor is it guaranteed to last. It requires diligence, discipline, and a steadfast commitment to living in alignment with God's will. It is not about hoarding wealth for ourselves but rather about using our resources to uplift and empower others.

In the book of Proverbs, we are reminded that "the blessing of the Lord brings wealth, without painful toil for it." This is not to say that hard work and perseverance are not important, but rather that true prosperity comes from God's abundant grace and favor.

Prosperity is a state of being. Jesus warned us in John 10:10 that the adversary came to steal, kill and destroy but the Lord came that we might experience abundant life. Your breakthrough is on the horizon and great things are in store for you.

Remember, prosperity stretches into every part of your life. You prosper physically when you experience healthy, energetic days. You prosper spiritually when you are in covenant relationship with the Lord and know prayers are answered through your established level of intimacy with the Creator. You prosper financially when there is enough to pay debts, support the ministry and overflow to enjoy blessings in life. You prosper mentally when there is peace, joy and sanity throughout your days. There are many ways to prosper. The Lord wants you to experience great health and great wealth as you serve in the kingdom.

Today, let us evaluate the areas of our lives that need amendment and adjustment. Also, let us focus our prayers on the areas that we are seeking a greater level of anointing and advancement. As you prosper, God will enable you to take others to the level you have attained.

In your prayer time today, specifically: 1) Thank God for the ways you have prospered in the past, 2) Cancel every evil assignment to block your prosperity, peace and power, and 3) Release abundance and overflow for you and generations to come.

Living in prosperity also means cultivating an attitude of gratitude and contentment, while recognizing and appreciating the blessings that we have been given, rather than constantly striving for more. It is about finding joy and fulfillment in the simple pleasures of life and being grateful for the abundance that surrounds us.

But perhaps most importantly, living in prosperity requires us to be good stewards of God's blessings, using them wisely and generously for the betterment of our communities and the world. As Jesus taught us, "To whom much is given, much will be required." (Luke 12:48)

So, my dear friends, let us embrace the blessings of prosperity with humility and gratitude, recognizing that they are gifts from a loving and generous God. Let us use our resources to serve others, to alleviate suffering, and to build a world where all can experience the fullness of life.

May we be inspired by the words of the psalmist, who declares, "The Lord will indeed give what is good, and our land will yield its harvest." (Psalm 85:12) May we live each day in the light of God's abundant blessings and may we share that abundance with all whom we encounter. Amen.

> Living in prosperity also means cultivating an attitude of gratitude and contentment, while recognizing and appreciating the blessings that we have been given.

> living in prosperity requires us to be good stewards of God's blessings, using them wisely and generously for the betterment of our communities and the world.

PERSONAL TRANSFORMATION ASSIGNMENT

1. Read Psalm 122:7 and write your interpretation of this scripture.

   _____

   _____

2. What does Proverbs 28:25 mean to you at this stage of your life?

   _____

   _____

3. Name a biblical character that prospered in at least one area of their life. Name the evidence of prosperity.

   _____

   _____

4. Name things that block our prosperity in life

   _____

   _____

5. Name the areas you are asking God to prosper in your life this year.

   _____

   _____

6. What are evidences of prosperity in the natural realm?

   _____

   _____

7. What has been the most thought-provoking part of this lesson?

8. What advice would you give to a person who wants to prosper but doesn't want to work for it?

    _____

    _____

9. Name three ways you can apply today's lesson to your life.

    _____

    _____

10. Write five people that you will ask God to prosper this year.

    _____

    _____

11. Write a prayer or poem you will recite when you need a financial breakthrough.

    _____

    _____

12. Spend time in prayer, asking God to lead you in the path of prosperity. Write the areas of your life where you are seeking prosperity.

    _____

    _____

PRAYER

Dear Lord, please continue to purge negativity from my life and prosper all that I do for your kingdom in the name of Jesus, Amen.

JOURNAL ENTRY

(Please use this space or your own book designated for this time.)

Dear Lord, my life is

_____

_____

_____

_____

I need the Holy Spirit to

_____

_____

_____

_____

Please bless me to

_____

_____

_____

_____

Today, I have been transformed by

_____

_____

_____

_____

"God wants you to get where God wants you to go more than you want to get where God wants you to go."

— **Mark Batterson,**
In a Pit with a Lion on a Snowy Day:
How to Survive and Thrive When Opportunity Roars

Day Fifteen

<hr/>

Word for the day: **PROMISE**

Dear Journey Partner,

It's the beginning of the third week of our life upgrade process! You have come a great way and there is much in store for your faith, finance and future. The Lord is in control and will bless you abundantly, as you place your faith in God and await the manifestation of divine promises. Today, we are reminded of the promises of God and how the promises will be kept during our journey and especially in this new season and year of your life. Great things are about to happen. Why? Because God said so.

Greater is coming!

Pastor D

BIBLICAL PASSAGES

Memory Verse: "Let us hold tightly without wavering to the hope we affirm, for God can be trusted to keep his promise" (Hebrews 10:23 NLT).

"So now there is no condemnation for those who belong to Christ Jesus. For the power of the life-giving Spirit has freed you through Christ Jesus from the power of sin that leads to death. The law of Moses could not save us, because of our sinful nature. But God put into effect a different plan to save us. He sent his own Son in a human body like ours, except that ours are sinful. God destroyed sin's control over us by giving his Son as a sacrifice for our sins. He did this so that the requirement of the law would be fully accomplished for us who no longer follow our sinful nature but instead follow the Spirit. Those who are dominated by the sinful nature think about sinful things, but those who are controlled by the Holy Spirit think about things that please the Spirit. If your sinful nature controls your mind, there is death. But if the Holy Spirit controls your mind, there is life and peace. For the sinful nature is always hostile to God. It never did obey God's laws, and it never will. That's why those who are still under the control of their sinful nature can never please God. But you are not controlled by your sinful nature. You are controlled by the Spirit if you have the Spirit of God living in you. (And remember that those who do not have the Spirit of Christ living in them are not Christians at all.) Since Christ lives within you, even though your body will die because of sin, your spirit is alive because you have been made right with God. The Spirit of God, who raised Jesus from the dead, lives in you. And just as he raised Christ from the dead, he will give life to your mortal body by this same Spirit living within you. So, dear brothers and sisters, you have no obligation whatsoever to do what your sinful nature urges you to do. For if you keep on following it, you will perish. But if through the power of the Holy Spirit you turn from it and its evil deeds, you will live. For all who are led by the Spirit of God are children of God. So you should not be like cowering, fearful slaves.

You should behave instead like God's very own children, adopted into his family — calling him 'Father, dear Father.' For his Holy Spirit speaks to us deep in our hearts and tells us that we are God's children. And since we are his children, we will share his treasures — for everything God gives to his Son, Christ, is ours, too. But if we are to share his glory, we must also share his suffering. Yet what we suffer now is nothing compared to the glory he will give us later. For all creation is waiting eagerly for that future day when God will reveal who his children really are. Against its will, everything on earth was subjected to God's curse. All creation anticipates the day when it will join God's children in glorious freedom from death and decay. For we know that all creation has been groaning as in the pains of childbirth right up to the present time. And even we Christians, although we have the Holy Spirit within us as a foretaste of future glory, also groan to be released from pain and suffering. We, too, wait anxiously for that day when God will give us our full rights as his children, including the new bodies he has promised us. Now that we are saved, we eagerly look forward to this freedom. For if you already have something, you don't need to hope for it. But if we look forward to something we don't have yet, we must wait patiently and confidently. And the Holy Spirit helps us in our distress. For we don't even know what we should pray for, nor how we should pray. But the Holy Spirit prays for us with groanings that cannot be expressed in words. And the Father who knows all hearts knows what the Spirit is saying, for the Spirit pleads for us believers in harmony with God's own will. And we know that God causes everything to work together for the good of those who love God and are called according to his purpose for them. For God knew his people in advance, and he chose them to become like his Son, so that his Son would be the firstborn, with many brothers and sisters. And having chosen them, he called them to come to him. And he gave them right standing with himself, and he promised them his glory. What can we say about such wonderful things as these? If God is for us, who can ever be against us? Since God did not spare even his own Son but gave him up for us all, won't God, who gave us

Christ, also give us everything else? Who dares accuse us whom God has chosen for his own? Will God? No! He is the one who has given us right standing with himself. Who then will condemn us? Will Christ Jesus? No, for he is the one who died for us and was raised to life for us and is sitting at the place of highest honor next to God, pleading for us. Can anything ever separate us from Christ's love? Does it mean he no longer loves us if we have trouble or calamity, or are persecuted, or are hungry or cold or in danger or threatened with death? (Even the Scriptures say, 'For your sake we are killed every day; we are being slaughtered like sheep.') No, despite all these things, overwhelming victory is ours through Christ, who loved us. And I am convinced that nothing can ever separate us from his love. Death can't, and life can't. The angels can't, and the demons can't. Our fears for today, our worries about tomorrow, and even the powers of hell can't keep God's love away. Whether we are high above the sky or in the deepest ocean, nothing in all creation will ever be able to separate us from the love of God that is revealed in Christ Jesus our Lord" (Romans 8).

"Listen in silence before me, you lands beyond the sea. Bring your strongest arguments. Come now and speak. The court is ready for your case. Who has stirred up this king from the east, who meets victory at every step? Who, indeed, but the LORD? He gives him victory over many nations and permits him to trample their kings underfoot. He puts entire armies to the sword. He scatters them in the wind with his bow. He chases them away and goes on safely, though he is walking over unfamiliar ground. Who has done such mighty deeds, directing the affairs of the human race as each new generation marches by? It is I, the LORD, the First and the Last. I alone am he. The lands beyond the sea watch in fear. Remote lands tremble and mobilize for war. They encourage one another with the words, 'Be strong!' The craftsmen rush to make new idols. The carver hurries the goldsmith, and the molder helps at the anvil. 'Good,' they say. 'It's coming along fine.' Carefully they join the parts together, then fasten the thing in place so it won't fall over. 'But as for you, Israel my servant, Jacob my chosen one, descended from my friend Abraham, I have called you back from the ends of the earth so you can serve me. For I have chosen you and will not throw you away. Don't be afraid, for I am with you. Do not be dismayed, for I am your God. I will strengthen you. I will help you. I will uphold you with my victorious right hand. See, all your angry enemies lie there, confused and ashamed. Anyone who opposes you will die. You will look for them in vain. They will all be gone! I am holding you by your right hand — I, the LORD your God. And I say to you, 'Do not be afraid. I am here to help you. Despised though you are, O Israel, don't be afraid, for I will help you. I am the LORD, your Redeemer. I am the Holy One of Israel.' You will be a new threshing instrument with many sharp teeth. You will tear all your enemies apart, making chaff of mountains. You will toss them in the air, and the wind will blow them all away; a whirlwind will scatter them. And the joy of the LORD will fill you to overflowing. You will glory in the Holy One of Israel. When the poor and needy search for water and there is none, and their tongues are parched from thirst, then I, the LORD, will answer them. I, the God of Israel, will never forsake them. I will open up rivers for them on high plateaus. I will give them fountains of water in the valleys. In the deserts they will find pools of water. Rivers fed by springs will flow across the dry, parched ground. I will plant trees — cedar, acacia, myrtle, olive, cypress, fir, and pine — on barren land. Everyone will see this miracle and understand that it is the LORD, the Holy One of Israel, who did it. Can your idols make such claims as these? Let them come and show what they can do! says the LORD, the King of Israel. Let them try to tell us what happened long ago or what the future holds. Yes, that's it! If you are gods, tell what will occur in the days ahead. Or perform a mighty miracle that will fill us with amazement and fear. Do something, whether good or bad! But no! You are less than nothing and can do nothing at all. Anyone who chooses you becomes filthy, just like you! But I have stirred up a leader from the north and east. He will come against the nations and call on my name, and I will give him victory over kings and princes. He will trample them as a potter treads on clay. Who but I have told you this would happen? Who else predicted this, making you admit that he was right? No one else said a word! I was the first to tell Jerusalem, 'Look! Help is on the way!' Not one of your idols told you this. Not one gave any answer when I asked. See, they are all foolish, worthless things. Your idols are all as empty as the wind" (Isaiah 41)."When Moses had finished saying these things to all the people of Israel, he said, 'I am now 120 years old and am no longer able to lead you. The LORD has told me that I will not cross the Jordan River. But the LORD your God himself will cross over ahead of you. He will destroy the nations living there, and you will take possession of their land. Joshua is your new leader, and he will go with you, just as the LORD promised. The LORD will destroy the nations living in the land, just as he destroyed Sihon and Og, the kings of the Amorites. The LORD will hand over to you the people who live there, and you will deal with them as I have commanded you. Be strong and courageous! Do not be afraid of them! The LORD your God will go ahead of you. He will neither fail you nor forsake you.' Then Moses called for Joshua, and as all Israel watched he said to him, 'Be strong and courageous! For you will lead these people into the land that the LORD swore to give their ancestors. You are the one who will deliver it to them as their inheritance. Do not be afraid or discouraged, for the LORD is the one who goes before you. He will be with you; he will neither fail you nor forsake you'" (Deuteronomy 31:1-8).

PERSONAL ASSESSMENT

1. What is a promise?

   _____

   _____

2. Do people keep their promises to you? Why or why not?

   _____

   _____

3. Do you keep your promises to others? Why or why not?

   _____

   _____

4. What broken promises do you remember in your life?

   _____

   _____

5. What promises are you seeking God for currently?

   _____

   _____

LIFE TRANSFORMATION MESSAGE

It is important to meditate on the promises of our faithful and loving God. In a world filled with uncertainty and turmoil, we find solace and strength in the unwavering assurances that God has given us. From the beginning of time, God has been making promises to God's people – promises of love, provision, protection, and salvation. These promises are not empty words but firm declarations of God's unchanging character and boundless compassion for His children.

In the book of Isaiah, God declares, "So do not fear, for I am with you; do not be dismayed, for I am your God. I will strengthen you and help you; I will uphold you with my righteous right hand." What a powerful assurance we have that God is always by our side, ready to uphold and sustain us in times of need.

Throughout the pages of Scripture, we see countless examples of God's faithfulness in fulfilling God's promises. From the covenant God made with Abraham to bless all nations through God's descendants, to the promise of a Savior who would redeem humanity from sin and death, God has never failed to keep divine promises. Furthermore, God's promises are not confined to the pages of ancient texts – they are alive and active in our lives today. God promises to never leave us nor forsake us, to give us strength when we are weak, and to guide us along the path of righteousness.

> God has never failed to keep divine promises.

In the midst of life's trials and tribulations, let us hold fast to the promises of God and trust in the unfailing love. Even when the storms rage and the winds howl, God remains steadfast and true, a rock of refuge for all who take refuge in God. As the psalmist declares, "The Lord is trustworthy in all He promises and faithful in all He does." (Psalm 145:13) Let us, therefore, anchor our souls in the promises of God, knowing that God who has promised is faithful.

You are in a covenant relationship with the Lord. In this relationship, God has made promises to you, and you make promises to God. There are many biblical promises that we can pray and hold on to during our times of storm and transition in life. The Lord has promised to always be with you, lead you on the path designed for you, cover your family, heal your diseases, bless your offspring and so much more. Throughout the sacred texts, there is evidence of the Lord keeping promises and yielding more than ever imagined for His people. The examples are numerous, and the products are actual. You are an addition to that number as God continually demonstrates faithfulness in your life.

Today, I want to remind you that you are on this journey because of the call of God on your life to lead you into visions, dreams and goals. You will realize them and you will attain all that God has in store for you because the Lord is a promise keeper. The ultimate will of God includes your prosperity, provision and promise.

The ultimate will of God includes your prosperity, provision and promise.

Regardless of what you face from day to day, the Lord will bless, keep, anoint, save and deliver those who confess and believe. God made those promises to our ancestors and continues to shower love and care upon us now and forever.

Today, centralize your focus on the promises of God. Remember God will bring you through everything God brought you to. It's your season to move forward and you will reach a higher level in the path for you. Greater is coming!

God will bring you through everything God brought you to..

May we draw comfort and strength from the promises of our Creator, and may our trust in God be unwavering, knowing that God is faithful to fulfill all that He has spoken. Amen.

PERSONAL TRANSFORMATION ASSIGNMENT

1. Read John 6:37 and write your interpretation of this scripture.

     _____

     _____

2. What does 1 John 1:9 mean to you at this stage of your life?

     _____

     _____

3. Name a biblical character that received the promises of God in their life.

     _____

     _____

4. Name the promises of God that are manifest in your life.

     _____

     _____

5. Write three points that you learned from the scriptural readings for today.

     _____

     _____

6. What promises were made in Romans 8?

     _____

     _____

7. How long did it take for the children of Israel to walk in their promise?

     _____

     _____

8. What advice would you give to the person who wants to hold on to the promises of God?

_____

_____

9. Name three ways you can apply today's lesson to your life.

_____

_____

10. Write five promises that you will keep toward God and others this year.

_____

_____

11. Write a prayer of thanksgiving to the Lord for keeping His promises to you.

_____

_____

12. Spend time in prayer, asking God to lead you in the promises you should make to others and yourself this year.

_____

_____

PRAYER

Dear Lord, thank you for keeping your promises and revealing your will in my life continually. Please continue to show me your glory in all aspects of my life, in the name of Jesus, Amen.

JOURNAL ENTRY

(Please use this space or your own book designated for this time.)

Dear Lord, thank you for

_____

_____

_____

_____

I solemnly promise to

_____

_____

_____

_____

I forgive

_____

_____

_____

_____

Today, I have been transformed by

_____

_____

_____

_____

"Patience strengthens the spirit, sweetens the temper, stifles anger, extinguishes envy, subdues pride, bridles the tongue."
— George Horne

Day Sixteen

Word for the day: **PATIENCE**

Dear Journey Partner,

Your visions, dreams and goals are closer than ever before. God has placed the right people in position, and the provision is on the way for the realization and manifestation. What must you do? Wait on God! Do not rush – everything must be in place according to God's plan, will and timing. Allow the Lord to work miracles throughout the waiting process and the future testimony will exceed your expectations.

Greater is coming!

Pastor D

BIBLICAL PASSAGES

Memory Verse: "The end of a matter is better than its beginning, and patience is better than pride" (Ecclesiastes 7:8 NIV).

"The LORD is slow to anger and abounding in steadfast love, forgiving iniquity and transgression, but he will by no means clear the guilty, visiting the iniquity of the fathers on the children, to the third and the fourth generation" (KJV). (Numbers 14:18)

"But thou, O Lord, art a God full of compassion, and gracious, long suffering, and plenteous in mercy and truth" (KJV). (Psalms 86:15)

"The LORD is slow to anger and great in power, and the LORD will by no means clear the guilty. His way is in whirlwind and storm, and the clouds are the dust of his feet." (Nahum 1:3)

"Do you suppose, O man—you who judge those who practice such things and yet do them yourself—that you will escape the judgment of God? Or do you presume on the riches of his kindness and forbearance and patience, not knowing that God's kindness is meant to lead you to repentance?" (Romans 2:3-4)

"The Lord is not slow to fulfill his promise as some count slowness, but is patient toward you, not wishing that any should perish, but that all should reach repentance." (2 Peter 3:9)

"The signs of a true apostle were performed among you with utmost patience, with signs and wonders and mighty works." (2 Corinthians 12:12)

"But the fruit of the Spirit is love, joy, peace, patience, kindness, goodness, faithfulness, gentleness, self-control; against such things there is no law." (Galatians 5:22-23)

"I therefore, a prisoner for the Lord, urge you to walk in a manner worthy of the calling to which you have been called, with all humility and gentleness, with patience, bearing with one another in love, eager to maintain the unity of the Spirit in the bond of peace." (Ephesians 4:1-3)

"May you be strengthened with all power, according to his glorious might, for all endurance and patience with joy, giving thanks to the Father, who has qualified you to share in the inheritance of the saints in light." (Colossians 1:11-12)

"Put on then, as God's chosen ones, holy and beloved, compassionate hearts, kindness, humility, meekness, and patience, bearing with one another and, if one has a complaint against another, forgiving each other; as the Lord has forgiven you, so you also must forgive." (Colossians 3:12-13)

"... As for that in the good soil, they are those who, hearing the word, hold it fast in an honest and good heart, and bear fruit with patience." (Luke 8:15)

"He will render to each one according to his works: to those who by patience in well-doing seek for glory and honor and immortality, he will give eternal life..." (Romans 2:6-7)

"For in this hope we were saved. Now hope that is seen is not hope. For who hopes for what he sees? But if we hope for what we do not see, we wait for it with patience." (Romans 8:24-25)

"But I received mercy for this reason, that in me, as the foremost, Jesus Christ might display his perfect patience as an example to those who were to believe in him for eternal life." (1 Timothy 1:16)

"And we desire each one of you to show the same earnestness to have the full assurance of hope until the end, so that you may not be sluggish, but imitators of those who through faith and patience inherit the promises." (Hebrews 6:11-12)

PERSONAL ASSESSMENT

Give an honest assessment of yourself.

I am a loving person.	° Strongly agree ° Neutral	°Strongly disagree
I am patient.	° Strongly agree ° Neutral	°Strongly disagree
I don't mind waiting on God	° Strongly agree ° Neutral	°Strongly disagree.
I don't mind waiting on others.	° Strongly agree ° Neutral	°Strongly disagree
Quiet time is a normal part of my day.	° Strongly agree ° Neutral	°Strongly disagree
I will wait a year for my goal to be met.	° Strongly agree ° Neutral	°Strongly disagree
There's not enough time in the day.	° Strongly agree ° Neutral	°Strongly disagree

LIFE TRANSFORMATION MESSAGE

The virtue of patience is often elusive in our fast-paced and instant-gratification society. Patience, however, is not merely a passive waiting but an active and enduring trust in the timing and wisdom of God. In a world where everything seems to move at lightning speed, patience can feel like a rare and precious commodity. We live in an age of instant communication, fast food, and overnight delivery, where waiting even a few moments can test our patience and tolerance. But let us remember, my beloved, that patience is not a sign of weakness but of strength. It is the ability to remain steadfast in the face of adversity, to persevere through trials and tribulations, and to trust in God's perfect timing.

The Bible is replete with examples of patience and endurance, from the steadfast faith of Job in the midst of suffering to the long-awaited fulfillment of God's promise to Abraham and Sarah in their old age. In each of these stories, we see how patience is rewarded with blessings beyond measure.

In the book of James, we are reminded: "Consider it pure joy, my brothers and sisters, whenever you face trials of many kinds because you know that the testing of your faith produces perseverance." Patience, then, is not merely about enduring trials but about allowing them to shape and strengthen our character.

> Patience, then, is not merely about enduring trials but about allowing them to shape and strengthen our character.

There are times in our lives that we can see the goal ahead of us but must wait for the manifestation of God's promise or resources to line up in our lives.

In 2014, I went through a difficult pregnancy. I was ill before the pregnancy and experienced many days of pain, sickness and distress. In the beginning of the pregnancy, everything appeared to be fine. For the average person looking at me, you would have thought I was perfectly healthy. On the contrary, the doctors gave a negative report at every visit and I had tests and monitoring every week. I was told that one of us and possibly both of us would not make it through. It was a trying time for my family and me, but I held on to the promises of God. After the seasons of growth and labor, we were blessed with a heathy, little angel – Mycah Alexandrea.

During the pregnancy, on the surface everything looked well although there were intense moments during my mandatory bed rest and hospitalization. Regardless of what I endured, I had to wait those several months so the baby would reach an optimum stage of development and growth. I had to navigate through the pain and believe God instead of man. As I learned to be patient, the promise was manifested in my life in a greater way than any of us ever expected.

Similarly, my friend, there are things happening within your spirit during this journey. Others cannot see the obstacles and obstructions you have had to face. No one else will ever understand all that it took for you to endure and overcome. Yet, your patience through the process is making a way for your victorious life.

Do not rush the process. Allow time for the preparation to be made properly and for all things to align in your life. There are times that it may seem tedious, but there is a reason for everything you face and endure. There is a master plan for your life. Be patient and God will work everything together for your good.

"Timing is so important! If you are going to be successful in dance, you must be able to respond to rhythm and timing. It's the same in the Spirit. People who don't understand God's timing can become spiritually spastic, trying to make the right things happen at the wrong time. They don't get His rhythm – and everyone can tell they are out of step. They birth things prematurely, threatening the very lives of their God-given dreams." ~ T. D. Jakes

How do we cultivate patience in our daily lives? It begins with surrendering our own desires and agendas to the will of God, trusting that divine plans for us are far greater than anything we could imagine.

It requires us to practice mindfulness and presence, embracing each moment as a gift from God.

Patience also involves cultivating empathy and compassion for others, recognizing that everyone is on their own journey and may be struggling in ways we cannot see. It is about extending grace and understanding, even when we are tempted to react with frustration or anger.

So, my dear friends, let us embrace the virtue of patience as we journey through life's ups and downs. Let us trust in God's timing, knowing that He is always working for our good, even when we cannot see it.

> Trust in God's timing, knowing that He is always working for our good, even when we cannot see it.

May our patience be a testament to the transformative power of faith and perseverance. Amen.

PERSONAL TRANSFORMATION ASSIGNMENT

1. Read Psalm 37:7 and write your interpretation of this scripture.

   _____

   _____

2. What does James 5:7-8 mean to you at this stage of your life?

   _____

   _____

3. Name a biblical character that exercised patience in their life.

   _____

   _____

4. Name one time you exercised great patience.

   _____

   _____

5. Write three points that you learned from the scriptural readings for today.

   _____

   _____

6. How can a person develop more patience?

   _____

   _____

7. How is God developing patience in your situation?

   _____

   _____

8. What advice would you give to person that is struggling with being patient?

_____

_____

9. Name three ways you can apply today's lesson to your life.

_____

_____

10. Return to your materials from Day #9 and read the prayer you wrote for perseverance.

_____

_____

PRAYER

Dear Lord, I am grateful for the plan you have for my life which includes prosperity and a great promise. Please enable me to wait for your will and your timing. Lead me in the path to renew my strength in the process. In the name of Jesus, Amen.

JOURNAL ENTRY

(Please use this space or your own book designated for this time.)

This journey has impacted my life

_____

_____

_____

_____

I am sorry for the times I

_____

_____

_____

_____

I will exercise patience in

_____

_____

_____

_____

Today, I have been transformed by

_____

_____

_____

_____

"God has not promised skies always blue, flower-strewn pathways all our life through; God has not promised sun without rain, joy without sorrow, peace without pain. But God has promised strength for the day, rest for the labor, light for the way; grace for the trials, help from above, unfailing sympathy, undying love."

Dr. Gardner C. Taylor

Day Seventeen

Word for the day: **PROVISION**

Dear Journey Partner,

Today is our day to concentrate on provision. God will provide everything you need and all that is necessary to carry out the divine plan and purpose for your life.

Spend time with the Creator today, and trust that every detail of your life will be perfected according to divine order. Everything you need in all facets of life will be provided.

> God will provide everything you need and all that is necessary to carry out the divine plan and purpose for your life.

Rest assured in the knowledge that your upgrade is on the horizon. It is God's promise made in covenant relationship, which will never be broken.

Your upgrade is in progress. Greater is coming!

Pastor D

BIBLICAL PASSAGES

Memory Verse: "The end of a matter is better than its beginning, and patience is better than pride" (Ecclesiastes 7:8 NIV).

"I really don't need to write to you about this gift for the Christians in Jerusalem. For I know how eager you are to help, and I have been boasting to our friends in Macedonia that you Christians in Greece were ready to send an offering a year ago. In fact, it was your enthusiasm that stirred up many of them to begin helping. But I am sending these brothers just to be sure that you really are ready, as I told them you would be, with your money all collected. I don't want it to turn out that I was wrong in my boasting about you. I would be humiliated — and so would you — if some Macedonian Christians came with me, only to find that you still weren't ready after all I had told them! So I thought I should send these brothers ahead of me to make sure the gift you promised is ready. But I want it to be a willing gift, not one given under pressure. Remember this — a farmer who plants only a few seeds will get a small crop. But the one who plants generously will get a generous crop. You must each make up your own mind as to how much you should give. Don't give reluctantly or in response to pressure. For God loves the person who gives cheerfully. And God will generously provide all you need. Then you will always have everything you need and plenty left over to share with others. As the Scriptures say, 'Godly people give generously to the poor. Their good deeds will never be forgotten.' For God is the one who gives seed to the farmer and then bread to eat. In the same way, he will give you many opportunities to do good, and he will produce a great harvest of generosity in you. Yes, you will be enriched so that you can give even more generously. And when we take your gifts to those who need them, they will break out in thanksgiving to God. So two good things will happen — the needs of the Christians in Jerusalem will be met, and they will joyfully express their thanksgiving to God. You will be glorifying God through your generous gifts. For your generosity to them will prove that you are obedient to the Good News of Christ. And they will pray for you with deep affection because of the wonderful grace of God shown through you. Thank God for his Son — a gift too wonderful for words! (2 Corinthians 9)

"Meanwhile, the crowds grew until thousands were milling about and crushing each other. Jesus turned first to his disciples and warned them, 'Beware of the yeast of the Pharisees — beware of their hypocrisy. The time is coming when everything will be revealed; all that is secret will be made public. Whatever you have said in the dark will be heard in the light, and what you have whispered behind closed doors will be shouted from the housetops for all to hear!' "Dear friends, don't be afraid of those who want to kill you. They can only kill the body; they cannot do any more to you. But I'll tell you whom to fear. Fear God, who has the power to kill people and then throw them into hell. What is the price of five sparrows? A couple of pennies? Yet God does not forget a single one of them. And the very hairs on your head are all numbered. So don't be afraid; you are more valuable to him than a whole flock of sparrows. And I assure you of this: If anyone acknowledges me publicly here on earth, I, the Son of Man, will openly acknowledge that person in the presence of God's angels if anyone denies me here on earth, I will deny that person before God's angels. Yet those who speak against the Son of Man may be forgiven, but anyone who speaks blasphemies against the Holy Spirit will never be forgiven. And when you are brought to trial in the synagogues and before rulers and authorities, don't worry about what to say in your defense, for the Holy Spirit will teach you what needs to be said even as you are standing there.' Then someone called from the crowd, 'Teacher, please tell my brother to divide our father's estate with me.' Jesus replied, 'Friend, who made me a judge over you to decide such things as that?' Then he said, 'Beware! Don't be greedy for what you don't have. Real life is not measured by how much we own.' And he gave an illustration: 'A rich man had a fertile farm that produced fine crops. In fact, his barns were full to overflowing. So he said, 'I know! I'll tear down my barns and build bigger ones. Then I'll have room enough to store everything. And I'll sit back and say to myself, My friend, you have enough stored away for years to come. Now take it easy! Eat, drink, and be merry!' "But God said to him, 'You fool! You will die this very night. Then who will get it all?' "Yes, a person is a fool to store up earthly wealth but not have a rich relationship with God.' Then turning to his disciples, Jesus said, 'So I tell you, don't worry about everyday life — whether you have enough food to eat or clothes to wear. For life consists of far more than food and clothing. Look at the ravens. They don't need to plant or harvest or put food in barns because God feeds them. And you are far more valuable to him than any birds! Can all your worries add a single moment to your life? Of course not! And if worry can't do little things like that, what's the use of worrying over bigger things? Look at the lilies and how they grow. They don't work or make their clothing, yet Solomon in all his glory was not dressed as beautifully as they are. And if God cares so wonderfully for flowers that are here today and gone tomorrow, won't he more surely care for you? You have so little faith! And don't worry about food — what to eat and drink. Don't worry whether God will provide it for you. These things dominate the thoughts of most people, but your Father already knows your needs. He will give you all you need from day to day if you make the Kingdom of God your primary concern. So don't be afraid, little flock. For it gives your Father great happiness to give you the Kingdom. Sell what you have and give to those in need. This will store up treasure for you in heaven! And the purses of heaven have no holes in them. Your treasure will be safe — no thief can steal it and no moth can destroy it. Wherever your treasure is, there your heart and thoughts will also be'" (Luke 12:1-34).

"Dear brothers and sisters, I love you and long to see you, for you are my joy and the reward for my work. So please stay true to the Lord, my dear friends. And now I want to plead with those two women, Euodia and Syntyche. Please, because you belong to the Lord, settle your disagreement. And I ask you, my true teammate, to help these women, for they worked hard with me in telling others the Good News. And they worked with Clement and the rest of my co-workers, whose names are written in the Book of Life. Always be full of joy in the Lord. I say it again — rejoice! Let everyone see that you are considerate in all you do. Remember, the Lord is coming soon. Don't worry about anything; instead, pray about everything. Tell God what you need, and thank him for all he has done. If you do this, you will experience God's peace, which is far more wonderful than the human mind can understand. His peace will guard your hearts and minds as you live in Christ Jesus. And now, dear brothers and sisters, let me say one more thing as I close this letter. Fix your thoughts on what is true and honorable and right. Think about things that are pure and lovely and admirable. Think about things that are excellent and worthy of praise. Keep putting into practice all you learned from me and heard from me and saw me doing, and the God of peace will be with you. How grateful I am, and how I praise the Lord that you are concerned about me again. I know you have always been concerned for me, but for a while you didn't have the chance to help me. Not that I was ever in need, for I have learned how to get along happily whether I have much or little. I know how to live on almost nothing or with everything. I have learned the secret of living in every situation, whether it is with a full stomach or empty, with plenty or little. For I can do everything with the help of Christ who gives me the strength I need. But even so, you have done well to share with me in my present difficulty. As you know, you Philippians were the only ones who gave me financial help when I brought you the Good News and then traveled on from Macedonia. No other church did this. Even when I was in Thessalonica you sent help more than once. I don't say this because I want a gift from you. What I want is for you to receive a well-earned reward because of your kindness. At the moment I have all I need — more than I need! I am generously supplied with the gifts you sent me with Epaphroditus. They are a sweet-smelling sacrifice that is acceptable to God and pleases him. And this same God who takes care of me will supply all your needs from his glorious riches, which have been given to us in Christ Jesus. Now glory be to God our Father forever and ever. Amen. Give my greetings to all the Christians there. The brothers who are with me here send you their greetings. And all the other Christians send their greetings, too, especially those who work in Caesar's palace. May the grace of the Lord Jesus Christ be with your spirit." (2 Corinthians 13:14)

PERSONAL ASSESSMENT

1. What is the vision God has given you?
   _____

   _____

2. What kind of provision do you need for the vision?
   _____

   _____

3. Have you been a good steward of your time? How? How not?
   _____

   _____

4. Have you been a good steward of your money? How? How not?
   _____

   _____

5. Have you been a good steward of your energy? How? How not?
   _____

   _____

6. Are you a faithful tither? Why or why not?
   _____

   _____

LIFE TRANSFORMATION MESSAGE

From the beginning of time, God has been our faithful provider, meeting our needs and showering us with blessings beyond measure.

In the book of Matthew, Jesus reassures us, saying, "Therefore I tell you, do not worry about your life, what you will eat or drink; or about your body, what you will wear. Is not life more than food, and the body more than clothes? Look at the birds of the air; they do not sow or reap or store away in barns, and yet your heavenly Father feeds them. Are you not much more valuable than they?"

These words remind us of the abundant care and provision that God extends to all of creation. Just as God provides for the birds of the air and the lilies of the field, so, too, does God provide for each and every one of us, God's beloved children.

God's provision is not limited to our physical needs. God also provides for us spiritually, offering us grace, forgiveness, and eternal life through the Son, Jesus Christ. It is through Christ's sacrificial love that we are reconciled to God and granted the gift of salvation.

> Our Creator knows our needs before we even ask and is always faithful to provide for us in God's perfect timing.

In times of scarcity and want, it can be easy to succumb to fear and anxiety, to doubt God's faithfulness and provision. But let us be reminded that our Creator knows our needs before we even ask and is always faithful to provide for us in God's perfect timing.

As the psalmist declares, "The Lord is my shepherd, I lack nothing. He makes me lie down in green pastures, he leads me beside quiet waters, he refreshes my soul." (Psalm 23) What a beautiful image of God's abundant provision, leading us to places of peace and abundance, even in the midst of life's storms.

> The Lord will make provision for every vision.

The Lord will make provision for every vision. When God told the children of Israel to depart from Egypt, God already opened doors, seas and opportunities for their journey. God provided manna, water, shelter and assistance in every part of the trip until they reached the place of promise. Every need was provided for them and the Lord showered them with love and care.

Similarly, my journey partner, you are on a mission for the Lord. The dreams, visions and goals inside of you are bigger than you and more than you can afford or accomplish. It must be afforded supernaturally by the power of the Lord.

Today, it is important to work through some practical exercises as well as intimate prayers for the path you are on. The Lord will honor the written visions and expressed prayers. Be specific in your prayers and efforts and the Lord will provide bountifully for you and the many people that will be blessed through the fulfillment of God's perfect plan concerning you.

Remember, the Lord takes care of the lilies, ravens and sparrows… God will take care of you! You are God's chosen. Seek God's will and provision for the days ahead. Your dreams will be realized because the Lord will send the appropriate people, finance, resources and necessities to complete God's purposes through you. Greater is coming!

> Your dreams will be realized because the Lord will send the appropriate people, finance, resources and necessities to complete God's purposes through you.

So, let us trust in the provision of our God, knowing that He is always with us, guiding us, and providing for us in every season of life.

May we open our hearts to receive God's blessings with gratitude and humility, and may we be ever mindful of divine love and abundant grace. Amen.

PERSONAL TRANSFORMATION ASSIGNMENT

1. Read Psalm 34:10 and write your interpretation of this scripture.

   _____

   _____

2. What does Psalm 84:11 mean to you at this stage of your life?

   _____

   _____

3. Name a biblical character that received supernatural provision in their life.

   _____

   _____

4. 4. Name one time you received a major blessing from the Lord.

   _____

   _____

5. Write three ideas that you learned from the scriptural readings for today.

   _____

   _____

6. What improvements can you make in your life regarding being a good steward of your time, money and other resources?

   _____

   _____

7. Write a projected budget for the vision God has given you below. Remember to include a ten percent tithe to the Lord. Write the categories here.

     _____

     _____

8. Write down a sum total that you are believing God for in this season.

     _____

     _____

9. Write down all the areas that you are asking God to provide for you in this season.

     _____

     _____

10. What are the similarities between you and the children of Israel?

     _____

     _____

11. Remember the lesson on prosperity. What is the difference between prosperity and provision?

     _____

     _____

12. Read the prayer from Day #14 and meditate on what you cried out to the Lord.

     _____

     _____

PRAYER

Dear Lord, Thank you in advance for making provision for all of my needs and the visions you have placed in me. I trust you to provide in abundant ways, In the name of Jesus, Amen.

Things you are believing God for this year

Resource	Amount Necessary For Vision	Amount Necessary For Overflow
STAFF PERSONS/ SALARY		
BUILDING		
EDUCATIONAL SUPPLIES		
ONGOING SUPPLIES/ MONEY		

UPKEEP		
LEGAL EXPENSES/ START UP COSTS		
OTHER _____		
TOTAL	**TOTAL**	**TOTAL**

List of Staff Persons Necessary:

1. Title _____ Job Description _____

_____

2. Title _____ Job Description _____

_____

3. Title _____ Job Description _____

_____

4. Title _____ Job Description _____

_____

5. Title _____ Job Description _____

_____

JOURNAL ENTRY

(Please use this space or your own book designated for this time.)

Lord, I thank you for

_____

_____

_____

_____

Please release provision for

_____

_____

_____

_____

As I receive blessings, I will

_____

_____

_____

_____

Today, I have been transformed by

_____

_____

_____

_____

"Amazing Peace: A Christmas Poem"

Thunder rumbles in the mountain passes
and lightning rattles the eaves of our houses.
Flood waters await us in our avenues.
Snow falls upon snow, falls upon snow to avalanche
Over unprotected villages.

The sky slips low and grey and threatening.

We question ourselves. What have we done to so affront nature?
We worry, God. Are you there? Are you there really?
Does the covenant you made with us still hold?

Into this climate of fear and apprehension, Christmas enters,
Streaming lights of joy, ringing bells of hope
And singing carols of forgiveness high up in the bright air.
The world is encouraged to come away from rancor,
Come the way of friendship.

It is the Glad Season. Thunder ebbs to silence and lightning
sleeps quietly in the corner. Flood waters recede into memory.
Snow becomes a yielding cushion to aid us
As we make our way to higher ground.

Hope is born again in the faces of children.
It rides on the shoulders of our aged as they walk into their sunsets.
Hope spreads around the earth. Brightening all things,
Even hate which crouches breeding in dark corridors.

In our joy, we think we hear a whisper.
At first it is too soft. Then only half heard.

We listen carefully as it gathers strength. We hear a sweetness.
The word is Peace. It is loud now.
It is louder. Louder than the explosion of bombs.

We tremble at the sound. We are thrilled by its presence.
It is what we have hungered for. Not just the absence of war.
But, true Peace. A harmony of spirit, a comfort of courtesies.
Security for our beloveds and their beloveds.

We clap hands and welcome the Peace of Christmas.
We beckon this good season to wait a while with us.We, Baptist
and Buddhist, Methodist and Muslim, say come. Peace.

Come and fill us and our world with your majesty.
We, the Jew and the Jainist, the Catholic and the Confucian,
Implore you, to stay a while with us.
So we may learn by your shimmering light How to look
beyond complexion and see community.

It is Christmas time, a halting of hate time.

On this platform of peace, we can create a language
To translate ourselves to ourselves and to each other.

At this Holy Instant, we celebrate the Birth of Jesus Christ Into the
great religions of the world.
We jubilate the precious advent of trust. We shout
with glorious tongues at the coming of hope.
All the earth's tribes loosen their voices.
To celebrate the promise of Peace.

We, Angels and Mortal's, Believers and Non-Believers,
Look heavenward and speak the word aloud. Peace.

We look at our world and speak the word aloud. Peace.
We look at each other, then into ourselves
And we say without shyness or apology or hesitation.

Peace, My Brother. Peace, My Sister. Peace, My Soul."

—Maya Angelou, Amazing Peace: A Christmas Poem

Day Eighteen

Word for the day: **PEACE**

Dear Journey Partner,

The Lord is preparing you for a greater plateau in life. We have labored tirelessly in the last seventeen days ensuring that our focus is on the Lord's will and promise and following the divine plan. One of the main things you should experience continually is peace. The Lord wants you to have peace especially as you lunge forward into your destiny, knowing that God is taking care of every detail of your life.

———†———

God is taking care of every detail of your life.

———

One of the main ways the adversary attacks the children of God is to place confusion and/or uncertainty in their lives. In particular, the adversary would like to keep you angry, confused and bitter because it will prevent you from having a clear focus and plan in the days to come. You cannot allow this to happen in your life – there is greater on the horizon for you.

In recent days, you have written the vision, worked up a projected budget, sought the Lord for the necessary provision, prayed for prosperity and promised to persevere. Now, you must place it all in God's hands and allow God's peace to guide your thoughts, ways and life.

Be careful that your focus is on things that are important to the Lord. Do not allow anyone or anything to deter you from your place of promise or the path you are on. Keep your mind and heart on the blessings and will of the Lord.

As you read through the materials for today, please make note of the things that bring you peace as well as things that you can do to cultivate

231

peace for others. This is a reciprocal process. You can bless someone's life by sharing the peace God has deposited in your heart.

If you have a lot of confusion and uncertainty in your life presently, purpose to pray and release it to the Lord today. God can handle your present and propel you to a better future than you expect or believe.

Read the scriptures on peace whenever you have difficult moments and reflect on the power of the Lord in your life.

———✝———

God can handle your present and propel you to a better future than you expect or believe.

Greater is coming!

Pastor D

BIBLICAL PASSAGES

Memory Verse: "Turn away from evil and do good. Search for peace and work to maintain it" (Psalm 34:14).

"I have told you these things, so that in me you may have peace. In this world you will have trouble. But take heart! I have overcome the world" (John 16.33).

"So letting your sinful nature control your mind leads to death. But letting the Spirit control your mind leads to life and peace" (Romans 8:6).

"And let the peace that comes from Christ rule in your hearts. For as members of one body you are called to live in peace. And always be thankful" (Colossians 3:15).

"God is our refuge and strength, an ever-present help in trouble" (Psalms 46:1).

"It is God who arms me with strength and makes my way perfect. He makes my feet like the feet of a deer; he enables me to stand on the heights. He trains my hands for battle; my arms can bend a bow of bronze. You give me your shield of victory, and your right hand sustains me; you stoop down to make me great. You broaden the path beneath me, so that my ankles do not turn" (Psalm 18:32-36).

"Great peace have those who love your law, and nothing can make them stumble" (Psalm 119:165).

"So do not fear, for I am with you; do not be dismayed, for I am your God. I will strengthen you and help you; I will uphold you with my righteous right hand" (Isaiah 41:10).

"Be strong and courageous. Do not be afraid or terrified because of them, for the Lord your God goes with you; he will never leave you nor forsake you" (Deuteronomy 31:6).

"But the fruit of the Spirit is love, joy, peace, patience, kindness, goodness, faithfulness, gentleness, self-control. Against such there is no law. And those who are Christ's have crucified the flesh with its passions and desires. If we all live in the Spirit, let us also walk in the Spirit. Let us not become conceited, provoking one another, envying one another" (Galatians 5:22-26).

"Peace I leave with you; my peace I give you. I do not give to you as the world gives. Do not let your hearts be troubled and do not be afraid" (John 14.27).

"May our Lord Jesus Christ himself and God our Father, who loved us and by his grace gave us eternal encouragement and good hope, encourage your hearts and strengthen you in every good deed and word" (2 Thessalonians 2:16-17).

"The Lord turn his face toward you and give you peace" (Numbers 6:26).

"Lord, you have assigned me my portion and my cup; you have made my lot secure. The boundary lines have fallen for me in pleasant places; surely I have a delightful inheritance. I will praise the Lord, who counsels me; even at night my heart instructs me. I have set the Lord always before me. Because he is at my right hand, I will not be shaken" (Psalm 16:5-8).

"The Lord gives his people strength. The Lord blesses them with peace" (Psalm 29:11).

"The Lord is my light and my salvation – whom shall I fear? The Lord is the stronghold of my life – of whom shall I be afraid?" (Psalm 27:1)

"Do not be anxious about anything, but in every situation, by prayer and petition, with thanksgiving, present your requests to God. And the peace of God, which transcends all understanding, will guard your hearts and your minds in Christ Jesus" (Philippians 4:6-7).

"For God has not given us a spirit of fear and timidity, but of power, love, and self-discipline" (2 Timothy 1:7).

"Therefore, since we have been made right in God's sight by faith, we have peace with God because of what Jesus Christ our Lord has done for us" (Romans 5:1).

"May the God of hope fill you all with joy and peace in believing, so that by the power of the Holy Spirit you may abound in hope" (Romans 15:13).

"Jesus Christ is the same yesterday and today and forever" (Hebrews 13:8).

"Do not let your hearts be troubled. Trust in God; trust also in me. In my Father's house are many rooms; if it were not so, I would have told you. I am going there to prepare a place for you. And if I go and prepare a place for you, I will come back and take you to be with me that you also may be where I am" (John 14:1-3).

"Cast your burden on the Lord, and he shall sustain you: he shall never suffer the righteous to be moved" (Psalms 55:22).

"So we do not lose heart. Though our outer self is wasting away, our inner self is being renewed day by day. For this light momentary affliction is preparing for us an eternal weight of glory beyond all comparison, as we look not to the things that are seen but to the things that are unseen. For the things that are seen are transient, but the things that are unseen are eternal" (Corinthians 4:16-18).

"He has made everything beautiful in its time. He has also set eternity in the hearts of men; yet they cannot fathom what God has done from beginning to end" (Ecclesiastes 3:11).

"May the Lord of peace himself give you peace at all times and in every way. The Lord be with all of you" (2 Thessalonians 3:16).

PERSONAL ASSESSMENT

1. What is your definition of peace?

2. Are you living a peaceful life? Why or why not?

3. What do you believe will help to cultivate peace in your life?

4. Do you bring peace to others' lives?

5. How do you deal with confusion?

LIFE TRANSFORMATION MESSAGE

———————†———————

A gift that is often overlooked in our fast-paced and chaotic world is the gift of peace. In a time where conflict, anxiety, and stress seem to dominate our lives, the pursuit of peace has never been more crucial. Peace is not merely the absence of conflict, but a profound sense of well-being and harmony that touches every aspect of our lives.

> Peace is not merely the absence of conflict, but a profound sense of well-being and harmony that touches every aspect of our lives.

First and foremost, true peace begins with our relationship with God. In Romans 5:1, Paul writes, "Therefore, since we have been justified through faith, we have peace with God through our Lord Jesus Christ." This peace with God is foundational; it is the reconciliation that Jesus Christ offers us through His sacrifice. When we accept His love and grace, we are no longer at odds with our Creator but are embraced as His children.

Once we have established peace with God, we can experience peace within ourselves. Philippians 4:6-7 encourages us, "Do not be anxious about anything, but in every situation, by prayer and petition, with thanksgiving, present your requests to God. And the peace of God, which transcends all understanding, will guard your hearts and your minds in Christ Jesus." This inner peace is a divine tranquility that surpasses our human comprehension, a calm in the storm of life's troubles.

Our inner peace should naturally extend to our relationships with others. Jesus emphasized the importance of peacemaking in the Beatitudes, saying, "Blessed are the peacemakers, for they will be called children of God" (Matthew 5:9). We are called to be ambassadors of peace, fostering reconciliation and harmony in our families, communities, and the world. This means listening with empathy, forgiving generously, and loving unconditionally.

When we embrace peace in our lives, it transforms us and those around us. The fruits of the Spirit listed in Galatians 5:22-23—love, joy, peace, patience, kindness, goodness, faithfulness, gentleness, and self-control—become evident in our daily interactions. A peaceful heart promotes a healthy body and mind, reduces stress, and cultivates a positive environment.

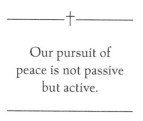

Our pursuit of peace is not passive but active.

In a world filled with turmoil and division, our pursuit of peace is not passive but active. Psalm 34:14 instructs us, "Turn from evil and do good; seek peace and pursue it." This requires us to engage with the world, to be agents of change, and to actively seek out ways to bring peace to every situation. Whether it's advocating for justice, offering a helping hand to those in need, or simply being a calming presence in a chaotic situation, our actions can make a significant difference.

Dear friends, let us strive to cultivate peace in every aspect of our lives. Let us start by nurturing our relationship with God, allowing divine peace to fill our hearts and minds. Let this peace overflow into our interactions with others, making us peacemakers in a world that desperately needs harmony and reconciliation. Remember, peace is not the absence of challenges but the presence of God's tranquility amidst them.

Peace is not the absence of challenges but the presence of God's tranquility amidst them.

May the peace of Christ be with you all, guiding you and guarding you every step of the way. Amen.

PERSONAL TRANSFORMATION ASSIGNMENT

1. Read Proverbs 14:30 and write your interpretation of this scripture.

   _____

   _____

2. What does Isaiah 54:13 mean to you at this stage of your life?

   _____

   _____

3. Name a biblical character that experienced peace in their life.

   _____

   _____

4. Name the things that cause confusion in your mind or spirit.

   _____

   _____

5. Write three points that you learned from the scriptural readings for today.

   _____

   _____

6. What improvements can you make in your life so you can focus on peace?

   _____

   _____

7. Read Proverbs 14:3. Make it personal by writing it here with your name inserted.

   _____

   _____

8. What are you releasing to the Lord today?

_____

_____

9. Write down ten things that bring peace to your life.

_____

_____

10. Make time for at least two of these things from #9 in the next seven days.

_____

_____

PRAYER

Dear Lord, Thank you for establishing peace in my life. Help me to seek your peace and to cultivate peace for others. In the name of Jesus, Amen

JOURNAL ENTRY

(Please use this space or your own book designated for this time.)

Today, I feel

_____

_____

_____

_____

I experience peace when

_____

_____

_____

_____

I am releasing

_____

_____

_____

_____

Today, I have been transformed by

_____

_____

_____

_____

"Every great dream begins with a dreamer.
Always remember, you have within you the strength, the patience,
and the passion to reach for the stars to change the world."
— Harriet Tubman

Day Nineteen

<<<<<<<<<<<<<<<<<<<<<<<<<<<<<<<<<<<<<<<<<<<<<<<<<<<<<<<<<<<<<<<<<<<<<<<<<<<<<<<<<<<<<<<<<<<<<<<<<<<<<<<<<<<<<<<<

Word for the day: **PROCLAMATION**

Dear Journey Partner,

As you go higher, it will be important to give ALL glory and honor to the Lord! Remember to place God first and to share your testimony with others. God uses us to bless others and provide strength through the journey. Today, ask the Lord for ways you can proclaim the wondrous acts and contribute more to the kingdom.

Greater is coming!

Pastor D

BIBLICAL PASSAGES

Memory Verse: "Oh give thanks to the Lord, call upon his name; Make known his deeds among the peoples" (Psalm 105:1).

"For I proclaim the name of the LORD; Ascribe greatness to our God! (Deuteronomy 32:3)

"I will not die, but live, and tell of the works of the LORD" (Psalms 118:17).

"He took this from their hand, and fashioned it with a graving tool and made it into a molten calf; and they said, 'This is your god, O Israel, who brought you up from the land of Egypt'" (Exodus 32:4).

"Speak to the sons of Israel and say to them, 'The LORD'S appointed times which you shall proclaim as holy convocations—My appointed times are these'" (Leviticus 23:2).

"You shall thus consecrate the fiftieth year and proclaim a release through the land to all its inhabitants It shall be a jubilee for you, and each of you shall return to his own property, and each of you shall return to his family" (Leviticus 25:10).

"Therefore thus says the LORD, 'You have not obeyed Me in proclaiming release each man to his brother and each man to his neighbor. Behold, I am proclaiming a release to you,' declares the LORD, 'to the sword, to the pestilence and to the famine; and I will make you a terror to all the kingdoms of the earth'" (Jeremiah 34:17).

"How lovely on the mountains Are the feet of him who brings good news, who announces peace and brings good news of happiness, who announces salvation, and says to Zion, 'Your God reigns!'" (Isaiah 52:7)

"For a voice declares from Dan and proclaims wickedness from Mount Ephraim" (Isaiah 52:7).

"And He said, 'I Myself will make all My goodness pass before you, and will proclaim the name of the LORD before you; and I will be gracious to whom I will be gracious, and will show compassion on whom I will show compassion'" (Exodus 33:19).

"Go and proclaim these words toward the north and say, 'Return, faithless Israel,' declares the LORD; 'I will not look upon you in anger For I am gracious,' declares the LORD; 'I will not be angry forever'" (Jeremiah 3:12).

"Behold, the LORD has proclaimed to the end of the earth, Say to the daughter of Zion, 'Lo, your salvation comes; Behold His reward is with Him, and His recompense before Him'" (Isaiah 62:11).

"What we have seen and heard we proclaim to you also, so that you too may have fellowship with us; and indeed our fellowship is with the Father, and with His Son Jesus Christ. These things we write, so that our joy may be made complete" (1 John 1:3-4).

PERSONAL ASSESSMENT

1. What is your definition of proclamation?

   _____

   _____

2. What do you share easily with others?

   _____

   _____

3. Is it easy for you to witness about God's grace?

   _____

   _____

4. How does God expect you to proclaim the gospel message in your life?

   _____

   _____

LIFE TRANSFORMATION MESSAGE

We celebrate the goodness and faithfulness of our gracious God and reflect on the power of positive proclamation in our lives. In a world often filled with negativity and despair, we are called to be beacons of hope, proclaiming the goodness of God and speaking life-giving words into every situation.

> We are called to be beacons of hope, proclaiming the goodness of God and speaking life-giving words into every situation.

The Bible tells us, "Death and life are in the power of the tongue, and those who love it will eat its fruits" (Proverbs 18:21). Our words have the power to shape our reality, to bring about change, and to align our hearts with the will of God. When we speak positively and proclaim God's goodness, we invite His blessings to flow into every area of our lives.

In the book of Psalms, we are encouraged to "taste and see that the Lord is good; blessed is the one who takes refuge in him" (Psalm 34:8). When we proclaim God's goodness, we are not only reminding our-selves of God's faithfulness, but we are also inviting others to experience His love and grace for themselves.

Speaking positively does not mean denying the challenges and struggles that we may face. Rather, it means choosing to focus on the promises of God and the hope that we have in God, even in the midst of adversity. It means declaring with confidence that God is at work in our lives, bringing about redemption and restoration.

The Lord has performed miracles and wonders in your life for a reason. You have been blessed so that you are a blessing to the kingdom of God. In everything you experience, it is important to share the good-ness, grace, love and peace of the Lord with others so they may be empowered for the journey.

When the Lord has blessed us abundantly, it is our responsibility to proclaim God's goodness to others. There are many people that will only know about God because of your spiritual relationship. Today, evaluate your life and the many things you can share to bless others.

The Lord heals some people so they can share God's miracle working power. The Lord gives bountifully to some, so they can express how God takes care of His own. The Lord grants you peace during turmoil so you can proclaim God's lovingkindness. Remember all that you have experienced. Do not live ashamed of your past; your testimony can help someone else to press forward into a great future.

As the Lord gives you "greater" in this season, God must be able to trust us to give all glory and honor back. Practice now with little beginnings and see how God blesses bountifully in the days to come.

> When we speak positively, we are planting seeds of faith and encouragement that have the power to bear fruit for generations to come.

As followers of Christ, we are called to be ambassadors of hope, proclaiming the good news of salvation and sharing the testimonies of God's faithfulness in our lives. When we speak positively, we are planting seeds of faith and encouragement that have the power to bear fruit for generations to come.

So, let us commit ourselves to proclaiming God's goodness and speaking positively in every circumstance. Let us declare with boldness that God is at work in our lives, transforming our trials into triumphs and our sorrows into joy. And may our words reflect the hope and love that we have found in Christ, shining brightly for all the world to see. Amen.

Share the gospel, share your testimony, share your faith – Greater is coming!

PERSONAL TRANSFORMATION ASSIGNMENT

1. Read Psalm 105 and write your interpretation of this scripture.

   _____

   _____

2. What does Exodus 33:19 mean to you at this stage of your life?

   _____

   _____

3. Name a biblical character that proclaimed the word of God in their life.

   _____

   _____

4. 4. Name ways to proclaim the word of God.

   _____

   _____

5. Write three points that you learned from the scriptural readings for today.

   _____

   _____

6. What improvements can you make in your life as you promise to proclaim?

   _____

   _____

7. Write down four things the Lord has done in your life recently.

   _____

   _____

8. Write a testimony you remember someone else sharing.

_____

_____

9. How did that testimony bless your life?

_____

_____

10. Name two people you will share a testimony with today.

_____

_____

11. Write the ways your vision will allow you to proclaim in the future.

_____

_____

12. Pray for a spirit of boldness and God's power to overshadow you.

_____

_____

PRAYER

Dear Lord, Thank you for blessing me in multiple ways throughout this season. Please lead me so I can proclaim your works and miracles to others. In the name of Jesus, Amen

JOURNAL ENTRY

(Please use this space or your own book designated for this time.)

The Lord has blessed me by

_____

_____

_____

_____

I share my testimony with others by

_____

_____

_____

_____

I remember when

_____

_____

_____

_____

Today, I have been transformed by

_____

_____

_____

_____

"The difference between a dreamer and a visionary is that a dreamer
has his eyes closed and a visionary has his eyes open"
Dr. Martin Luther King, Jr.

Day Twenty

Word for the day: **POSSIBILITIES**

Dear Journey Partner,

This time of journey has given you a new perspective, plan and level of power.

You are no longer limited by the narrow scope of the past; you have endless possibilities. No good thing will be withheld from you, and you will experience greater in abundance.

> ———†———
>
> You have endless possibilities.

Today, pause to think about your plans and continually look to the Lord for more. There is a plan to exceed every expectation and to build upon prior foundations to a higher level.

It's your time and season to experience supernatural overflow.

We trust and believe in God for the power, prosperity and provision assigned to your life. Greater is coming!

Greater is coming!

Pastor D

BIBLICAL PASSAGES

Memory Verse: "No eye has seen, no ear has heard, and no mind has imagined what God has prepared for those who love him" (1 Corinthians 2:9).

"Dear brothers and sisters, when I first came to you I didn't use lofty words and brilliant ideas to tell you God's message. For I decided to concentrate only on Jesus Christ and his death on the cross. I came to you in weakness — timid and trembling. And my message and my preaching were very plain. I did not use wise and persuasive speeches, but the Holy Spirit was powerful among you. I did this so that you might trust the power of God rather than human wisdom. Yet when I am among mature Christians, I do speak with words of wisdom, but not the kind of wisdom that belongs to this world, and not the kind that appeals to the rulers of this world, who are being brought to nothing. No, the wisdom we speak of is the secret wisdom of God, which was hidden in former times, though he made it for our benefit before the world began. But the rulers of this world have not understood it; if they had, they would never have crucified our glorious Lord. That is what the Scriptures mean when they say, 'No eye has seen, no ear has heard, and no mind has imagined what God has prepared for those who love him.' But we know these things because God has revealed them to us by his Spirit, and his Spirit searches out everything and shows us even God's deep secrets. No one can know what anyone else is really thinking except that person alone, and no one can know God's thoughts except God's own Spirit. And God has actually given us his Spirit (not the world's spirit) so we can know the wonderful things God has freely given us. When we tell you this, we do not use words of human wisdom. We speak words given to us by the Spirit, using the Spirit's words to explain spiritual truths. But people who aren't Christians can't understand these truths from God's Spirit. It all sounds foolish to them because only those who have the Spirit can understand what the Spirit means. We who have the Spirit understand these things, but others can't understand us at all. How could they? For, 'Who can know what the Lord is thinking? Who can give him counsel?' But we can understand these things, for we have the mind of Christ" (1 Corinthians 2).

"Whatever happens, dear brothers and sisters, may the Lord give you joy. I never get tired of telling you this. I am doing this for your own good. Watch out for those dogs, those wicked men and their evil deeds, those mutilators who say you must be circumcised to be saved. For we who worship God in the Spirit are the only ones who are truly circumcised. We put no confidence in human effort. Instead, we boast about what Christ Jesus has done for us. Yet I could have confidence in myself if anyone could. If others have reason for confidence in their own efforts, I have even more! For I was circumcised when I was eight days old, having been born into a pure-blooded Jewish family that is a branch of the tribe of Benjamin. So I am a real Jew if there ever was one! What's more, I was a member of the Pharisees, who demand the strictest obedience to the Jewish law. And zealous? Yes, in fact, I harshly persecuted the church. And I obeyed the Jewish law so carefully that I was never accused of any fault. I once thought all these things were so very important, but now I consider them worthless because of what Christ has done. Yes, everything else is worthless when compared with the priceless gain of knowing Christ Jesus my Lord. I have discarded everything else, counting it all as garbage, so that I may have Christ and become one with him. I no longer count on my own goodness or my ability to obey God's law, but I trust Christ to save me. For God's way of making us right with himself depends on faith. As a result, I can really know Christ and experience the mighty power that raised him from the dead. I can learn what it means to suffer with him, sharing in his death, so that, somehow, I can experience the resurrection from the dead! I don't mean to say that I have already achieved these things or that I have already reached perfection! But I keep working toward that day when I will finally be all that Christ Jesus saved me for and wants me to be. No, dear brothers and sisters, I am still not all I should be, but I am focusing all my energies on this one thing:

Forgetting the past and looking forward to what lies ahead, I strain to reach the end of the race and receive the prize for which God, through Christ Jesus, is calling us up to heaven. I hope all of you who are mature Christians will agree on these things. If you disagree on some point, I believe God will make it plain to you. But we must be sure to obey the truth we have learned already. Dear brothers and sisters, pattern your lives after mine, and learn from those who follow our example. For I have told you often before, and I say it again with tears in my eyes, that there are many whose conduct shows they are really enemies of the cross of Christ. Their future is eternal destruction. Their god is their appetite, they brag about shameful things, and all they think about is this life here on earth. But we are citizens of heaven, where the Lord Jesus Christ lives. And we are eagerly waiting for him to return as our Savior. He will take these weak mortal bodies of ours and change them into glorious bodies like his own, using the same mighty power that he will use to conquer everything, everywhere" (Philippians 3).

"This letter is from Jude, a slave of Jesus Christ and a brother of James. I am writing to all who are called to live in the love of God the Father and the care of Jesus Christ. May you receive more and more of God's mercy, peace, and love. Dearly loved friends, I had been eagerly planning to write to you about the salvation we all share. But now I find that I must write about something else, urging you to defend the truth of the Good News. God gave this unchanging truth once for all time to his holy people. I say this because some godless people have wormed their way in among you, saying that God's forgiveness allows us to live immoral lives. The fate of such people was determined long ago, for they have turned against our only Master and Lord, Jesus Christ. I must remind you — and you know it well — that even though the Lord rescued the whole nation of Israel from Egypt, he later destroyed every one of those who did not remain faithful. And I remind you of the angels who did not stay within the limits of authority God gave them but left the place where they belonged. God has kept them chained in prisons of darkness, waiting for the day of judgment. And don't forget the cities of Sodom and Gomorrah and their neighboring towns, which were filled with sexual immorality and every kind of sexual perversion. Those cities were destroyed by fire and are a warning of the eternal fire that will punish all who are evil. Yet these false teachers, who claim authority from their dreams, live immoral lives, defy authority, and scoff at the power of the glorious ones. But even Michael, one of the mightiest of the angels, did not dare accuse Satan of blasphemy, but simply said, 'The Lord rebuke you.' (This took place when Michael was arguing with Satan about Moses' body.) But these people mock and curse the things they do not understand. Like animals, they do whatever their instincts tell them, and they bring about their own destruction. How terrible it will be for them! For they follow the evil example of Cain, who killed his brother. Like Balaam, they will do anything for money. And like Korah, they will perish because of their rebellion. When these people join you in fellowship meals celebrating the love of the Lord, they are like dangerous reefs that can shipwreck you. They are shameless in the way they care only about themselves. They are like clouds blowing over dry land without giving rain, promising much but producing nothing. They are like trees without fruit at harvest time. They are not only dead but doubly dead, for they have been pulled out by the roots. They are like wild waves of the sea, churning up the dirty foam of their shameful deeds. They are wandering stars, heading for everlasting gloom and darkness. Now Enoch, who lived seven generations after Adam, prophesied about these people. He said, 'Look, the Lord is coming with thousands of his holy ones. He will bring the people of the world to judgment. He will convict the ungodly of all the evil things they have done in rebellion and of all the insults that godless sinners have spoken against him.' These people are grumblers and complainers, doing whatever evil they feel like. They are loudmouthed braggarts, and they flatter others to get favors in return. But you, my dear friends, must remember what the apostles of our Lord Jesus Christ told you, that in the last times there would be scoffers whose purpose in life is to enjoy themselves in every evil way imaginable. Now they are here, and they are the ones who are creating divisions among you. They live by natural instinct because they do not have God's Spirit living in them. But you, dear friends, must continue to build your lives on the foundation of your holy faith. And continue to pray as you are directed by the Holy Spirit. Live in such a way that God's love can bless you as you wait for the eternal life that our Lord Jesus Christ in his mercy is going to give you. Show mercy to those whose faith is wavering. Rescue others by snatching them from the flames of judgment. There are still others to whom you need to show mercy, but be careful that you aren't contaminated by their sins. And now, all glory to God, who is able to keep you from stumbling, and who will bring you into his glorious presence innocent of sin and with great joy. All glory to him, who alone is God our Savior, through Jesus Christ our Lord. Yes, glory, majesty, power, and authority belong to him, in the beginning, now, and forevermore. Amen" (Jude).

PERSONAL ASSESSMENT

1. How has this 21 Days of Personal Transformation improved
    your life?

    _____

    _____

2. What hopes and dreams are in your heart and spirit for the future?

    _____

    _____

3. Has your faith level increased? How or how not?

    _____

    _____

LIFE TRANSFORMATION MESSAGE

As we journey through life, it's easy to become ensnared by the limitations we perceive around us. We may feel confined by our circumstances, boxed in by our fears, or restricted by our past mistakes. But today, I want to remind you of a profound truth: there are unlimited possibilities in life.

When we look at the world through the lens of faith, we begin to see that our Creator is a God of boundless creativity and infinite potential. God is not constrained by the same limitations that we are. In fact, God's very nature is one of abundance and possibility.

In the book of Jeremiah, God declares, "For I know the plans I have for you, plans to prosper you and not to harm you, plans to give you hope and a future" (Jeremiah 29:11). These words remind us that God's plans for us are vast and expansive, far beyond anything we could ever imagine.

———+———

There are no limits to what God can accomplish through us when we surrender ourselves to the divine will.

As followers of Christ, we are called to embrace a mindset of abundance rather than scarcity. We serve a God who is able to do "immeasurably more than all we ask or imagine" (Ephesians 3:20). There are no limits to what God can accomplish through us when we surrender ourselves to the divine will.

I encourage you to dream big and bold dreams. Dare to believe

———+———

God has something extraordinary in store for your life.

that God has something extraordinary in store for your life. Step out in faith, trusting that God will guide your steps and open doors that no one can shut.

Remember, the possibilities are endless when we place our trust in the One who holds the universe in His hands. May you be filled with hope and excitement as you journey forward, knowing that with God, all things are possible.

May God bless you abundantly as you walk in faith and embrace the unlimited possibilities that await you. Amen.

PERSONAL TRANSFORMATION ASSIGNMENT

1. Read Philippians 3:13-14 and write your interpretation of this scripture.

   _____

   _____

2. What does Isaiah 43:19 mean to you at this stage of your life?

   _____

   _____

3. Name a biblical charac0ter that was blessed abundantly.

   _____

   _____

4. Write three points that you learned from the scriptural readings for today.

   _____

   _____

5. What areas do you believe God will allow you to experience super-natural overflow and possibilities?

   _____

   _____

6. What advice would you give to someone who has dreams that God could magnify?

   _____

   _____

7. Name a person you know that was blessed much more than they deserved.

_____

_____

8. How did that person's testimony bless your life?

_____

_____

9. Read your answer to #6 aloud and include your name in the advice.

_____

_____

10. Prepare a vision board for the future. Place pictures, scriptures and quotes on the timeline. Pray over this board each day for the next thirty days. Trust God for provision and prosperity.

_____

_____

PRAYER
Dear Lord, I am eternally grateful for your anointing in my life. Your plans for me exceed my thoughts and dreams, and I am honored to be your ambassador. Use me to bless others and advance the kingdom, in the name of Jesus, Amen

JOURNAL ENTRY

(Please use this space or your own book designated for this time.)

Lord, I am grateful for

_____

_____

_____

_____

I believe the Lord will

_____

_____

_____

_____

My future will be

_____

_____

_____

_____

Today, I have been transformed by

_____

_____

_____

_____

"Let men position you in the den, God will make you a Daniel in the den. Let men position you to face Goliath, God will make you a David. Let men subject you to undue pressure, torture and pain, blindfold you and lead you into the dungeon, God will make you a Samson there! Let men sell you into indentured servitude, God will make you Joseph. Let men build a death trap for you, God shall turn it into the days of Mordecai and Haman, and you shall only see with your eyes the destruction of evil conspirators who would never repent! Let all odds be against you, God will make you Job. And when though fear grips your heart because of the storm you see, God will empower you and make you more than Peter. Stay hopeful! Trust in God!"
— **Ernest Agyemang Yeboah**

Day Twenty-One

Word for the day: **POWER**

Dear Journey Partner,

Congratulations! You have made it to the twenty first day! You have demonstrated incredible patience, perseverance and purpose. Today, we will focus on the power of God which will be displayed in your life.

The Lord allowed you to journey through these twenty-one days as you developed a more intimate relationship with God and surrendered to God's ultimate will concerning you.

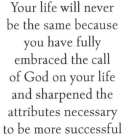

Your life will never be the same because you have fully embraced the call of God on your life and sharpened the attributes necessary to be more successful and excellent in all arenas.

There is great purpose and potential in you. Your life will never be the same because you have fully embraced the call of God on your life and sharpened the attributes necessary to be more successful and excellent in all arenas.

Let us remember today that every dream, vision and goal will be accomplished by the power of God.

You shall prosper as God provides all you need and more.

Ashe'. Amen. It is so.

Greater has come!

Pastor D

BIBLICAL PASSAGES

Memory Verse: "I pray that you will begin to understand the incredible greatness of his power for us who believe him. This is the same mighty power that raised Christ from the dead and seated him in the place of honor at God's right hand in the heavenly realms" (Ephesians 1:19-20).

"For Jeduthun, the choir director: A psalm of David. I wait quietly before God, for my salvation comes from him. He alone is my rock and my salvation, my fortress where I will never be shaken. So many enemies against one man — all of them trying to kill me. To them I'm just a broken-down wall or a tottering fence. They plan to topple me from my high position. They delight in telling lies about me. They are friendly to my face, but they curse me in their hearts. (Interlude) I wait quietly before God, for my hope is in him. He alone is my rock and my salvation, my fortress where I will not be shaken. My salvation and my honor come from God alone. He is my refuge, a rock where no enemy can reach me. O my people, trust in him at all times. Pour out your heart to him, for God is our refuge. Interlude From the greatest to the lowliest — all are nothing in his sight. If you weigh them on the scales, they are lighter than a puff of air. Don't try to get rich by extortion or robbery. And if your wealth increases, don't make it the center of your life. God has spoken plainly, and I have heard it many times: Power, O God, belongs to you; unfailing love, O Lord, is yours. Surely you judge all people according to what they have done" (Psalm 62).

"Hear the word of the LORD, O Israel! This is what the LORD says: 'Do not act like other nations who try to read their future in the stars. Do not be afraid of their predictions, even though other nations are terrified by them. Their ways are futile and foolish. They cut down a tree and carve an idol. They decorate it with gold and silver and then fasten it securely with hammer and nails so it won't fall over. There stands their god like a helpless scarecrow in a garden! It cannot speak, and it needs to be carried because it cannot walk. Do not be afraid of such gods, for they can neither harm you nor do you any good.' LORD, there is no one like you! For you are great, and your name is full of power. Who would not fear you, O King of nations? That title belongs to you alone! Among all the wise people of the earth and in all the kingdoms of the world, there is no one like you. The wisest of people who worship idols are stupid and foolish. The things they worship are made of wood! They bring beaten sheets of silver from Tarshish and gold from Uphaz, and they give these materials to skillful craftsmen who make their idols. Then they dress these gods in royal purple robes made by expert tailors. But the LORD is the only true God, the living God. He is the everlasting King! The whole earth trembles at his anger. The nations hide before his wrath. Say this to those who worship other gods: 'Your so-called gods, who did not make the heavens and earth, will vanish from the earth.' But God made the earth by his power, and he preserves it by his wisdom. He has stretched out the heavens by his understanding. When he speaks, there is thunder in the heavens. He causes the clouds to rise over the earth. He sends the lightning with the rain and releases the wind from his storehouses. Compared to him, all people are foolish and have no knowledge at all! They make idols, but the idols will disgrace their makers, for they are frauds. They have no life or power in them. Idols are worthless; they are lies! The time is coming when they will all be destroyed. But the God of Israel is no idol! He is the Creator of everything that exists, including Israel, his own special possession. The LORD Almighty is his name! 'Pack your bag and prepare to leave; the siege is about to begin,' says the LORD. 'For suddenly, I will fling you from this land and pour great troubles upon you. At last you will feel my anger.' My wound is desperate, and my grief is great. My sickness is incurable, but I must bear it. My home is gone, and no one is left to help me rebuild it. My children have been taken away, and I will never see them again. The shepherds of my people have lost their senses. They no longer follow the LORD or ask what he wants of them. Therefore, they fail completely, and their flocks are scattered. Listen! Hear the terrifying roar of great armies as they roll down from the north. The towns of Judah will be destroyed and will become a haunt for jackals. I know, LORD, that a person's life is not his own. No one is able to plan his own course. So correct me, LORD, but please be gentle. Do not correct me in anger, for I would die. Pour out your wrath on the nations that refuse to recognize you — on nations that do not call upon your name. For they have utterly devoured your people Israel, making the land a desolate wilderness" (Jeremiah 10).

"Children, obey your parents because you belong to the Lord, for this is the right thing to do. 'Honor your father and mother.' This is the first of the Ten Commandments that ends with a promise. And this is the promise: If you honor your father and mother, 'you will live a long life, full of blessing.' And now a word to you fathers. Don't make your children angry by the way you treat them. Rather, bring them up with the discipline and instruction approved by the Lord. Slaves, obey your earthly masters with deep respect and fear. Serve them sincerely as you would serve Christ. Work hard, but not just to please your masters when they are watching. As slaves of Christ, do the will of God with all your heart. Work with enthusiasm, as though you were working for the Lord rather than for people. Remember that the Lord will reward each one of us for the good we do, whether we are slaves or free. And in the same way, you masters must treat your slaves right. Don't threaten them; remember, you both have the same Master in heaven, and he has no favorites. A final word: Be strong with the Lord's mighty power. Put on all of God's armor so that you will be able to stand firm against all strategies and tricks of the Devil. For we are not fighting against people made of flesh and blood, but against the evil rulers and authorities of the unseen world, against those mighty powers of darkness who rule this world, and against wicked spirits in the heavenly realms. Use every piece of God's armor to resist the enemy in the time of evil, so that after the battle you will still be standing firm. Stand your ground, putting on the sturdy belt of truth and the body armor of God's righteousness. For shoes, put on the peace that comes from the Good News, so that you will be fully prepared. In every battle you will need faith as your shield to stop the fiery arrows aimed at you by Satan. Put on salvation as your helmet, and take the sword of the Spirit, which is the word of God. Pray at all times and on every occasion in the power of the Holy Spirit. Stay alert and be persistent in your prayers for all Christians everywhere. And pray for me, too. Ask God to give me the right words as I boldly explain God's secret plan that the Good News is for the Gentiles, too. I am in chains now for preaching this message as God's ambassador. But pray that I will keep on speaking boldly for him, as I should. Tychicus, a much loved brother and faithful helper in the Lord's work, will tell you all about how I am getting along. I am sending him to you for just this purpose. He will let you know how we are, and he will encourage you. May God give you peace, dear brothers and sisters, and love with faith, from God the Father and the Lord Jesus Christ. May God's grace be upon all who love our Lord Jesus Christ with an undying love" (Ephesians 6).

PERSONAL ASSESSMENT

1. How did you feel before this 21 Days of Personal Transformation?

   _____

   _____

2. How do you feel today?

   _____

   _____

3. Describe your current level of power.

   _____

   _____

LIFE TRANSFORMATION MESSAGE

There is a profound importance of relying on the power of God in our lives. In a world filled with uncertainty and challenges, it is easy to become overwhelmed and discouraged. But we are reminded time and time again throughout scripture that our strength does not come from ourselves but from the mighty power of our Creator.

In the book of Isaiah, we read, "Do you not know? Have you not heard? The Lord is the everlasting God, the Creator of the ends of the earth. He will not grow tired or weary, and his understanding no one can fathom. He gives strength to the weary and increases the power of the weak" (Isaiah 40:28-29). These words serve as a powerful reminder that God is our source of strength and power, and God is always ready to come to our aid when we call upon Him.

Too often, we rely on our own strength and abilities to navigate the challenges of life, only to find ourselves exhausted and defeated. But when we surrender ourselves to the power of God, we tap into a wellspring of infinite strength and wisdom that enables us to overcome even the greatest obstacles.

> When we surrender ourselves to the power of God, we tap into a wellspring of infinite strength and wisdom that enables us to overcome even the greatest obstacles.

Jesus Himself exemplified the importance of relying on the power of God during His time on earth. In the garden of Gethsemane, as He faced the prospect of His impending crucifixion, He prayed, "Father, if you are willing, take this cup from me; yet not my will, but yours be done" (Luke 22:42). In His moment of greatest weakness, Jesus turned to God for strength and guidance, trusting in His divine plan.

> God is with us, empowering us to live lives of purpose and fulfillment.

I encourage you to follow the example of our Savior and rely on the power of God in every aspect of our lives. Whether we are facing trials and tribulations or celebrating victories and blessings, let us always remember that God is with us, empowering us to live lives of purpose and fulfillment.

We have reached the closing days of this journey, which is a place to propel to divine destiny. Throughout this time and our closer walk with the Lord, we have learned not to limit the hand or power of God in our lives. Truly, the vision is bigger than we are and the plan exceeds our human limitations BUT, it does not exceed the miracle working power of our God. Our omnipotent God has all power!

You have turned your path, purpose and person over to the Lord. Now, it is time to let go and let God transform every thought and part into divine assignment and excellent greatness. You will exceed, overcome, excel and empower. It's not my word; it is the gospel truth from the word of God.

Be careful in the days ahead. Make sure you move forward, despite any issue or obstacle; make sure you acknowledge the Lord's power and sovereignty and above all else, grant all glory to the Lord. God is able and willing to bless you abundantly.

Today, we combine our *natural* with God's *super* and we will experience the **supernatural** power of God for all of the days of our lives.

Similar to the woman with an issue of blood, she wanted to be healed and when she asked for that, God forgave all diseases and realigned her with the Father. Her expectations were exceeded because she trusted God for the increase. You have asked God for great things in your walk with him, but I guarantee you, if you will only make this transformation experience a lifestyle change,

you will receive much, much more than you ever imagined.

There is a reason you are on this journey. You can no longer operate out of your own will and power. It's time to let God be the driving

"It is about the greatness of God, not the significance of man. God made man small and the universe big to say something about himself."

— **John Piper**

force in your life and world. God must be in chief control and then, God's blessings will be evident for the world to see through you.

Your latter shall be greater than your former. It is so and you will always walk in goodness and mercy until you reach the Heavenly gates. Then, you will hear your God say, "Well done, thy good and faithful servant."

As the Apostle Paul writes in his letter to the Ephesians, "Now to him who is able to do immeasurably more than all we ask or imagine, according to his power that is at work within us, to him be glory in the church and in Christ Jesus throughout all generations, for ever and ever! Amen" (Ephesians 3:20-21).

May we trust in the power of God, knowing that God is able to accomplish far more than we could ever ask or imagine. Amen.

PERSONAL TRANSFORMATION ASSIGNMENT

1. Read 2 Corinthians 6:7 and write your interpretation of this scripture.

   _____

   _____

2. What does Matthew 19:26 mean to you at this stage of your life?

   _____

   _____

3. Name a biblical character that received supernatural power from the Lord.

   _____

   _____

4. Write three main ideas that you learned from the scriptural readings for today.

   _____

   _____

5. In what areas are you seeking supernatural power?

   _____

   _____

6. Susan is a college educated woman that has lived an independent lifestyle with her two children. She operates with the mentality, "If you want something done well, you must do it yourself." Recently, she gave her life to the Lord and said she desires a closer walk with Him. What advice would you give Susan as she relies upon God's power?

   _____

   _____

7. Name a time you experienced the supernatural power of God in your life.

_____

_____

8. How did that situation change your life for the better?

_____

_____

9. Write two quotes or scriptures that remind you of the power of God.

_____

_____

10. If you could have only ten words in your obituary to describe you, what would you want them to be?

_____

_____

11. Read the following scriptures over the next week of your life: 1 Corinthians 4:20; Colossians 1:11; Job 12:13-16; 2 Samuel 22:23; Psalm 147:5 and Isaiah 40:29.

_____

_____

12. Write twenty-one ways your life has been transformed over the course of this journey.

_____

_____

1) _____

2) _____

3) _____

4) _____

5) _____

6) _____

7) _____

8) _____

9) _____

10) _____

11) _____

12) _____

13) _____

14) _____

15) _____

16) _____

17) _____

18) _____

19) _____

20) _____

21) _____

PRAYER

Almighty God, I am eternally grateful for this transformation experience and your miracle working power in my life. Help me to focus wholeheartedly on your plan and purpose for my life, as I cling to your promise and power, in the name of Jesus, Amen.

JOURNAL ENTRY

(Please use this space or your own book designated for this time.)

This journey has been

_____

_____

_____

_____

I have experienced supernatural power by

_____

_____

_____

_____

I am making the following lifestyle changes

_____

_____

_____

_____

Today, I have been transformed by

_____

_____

_____

_____

Upgrade Course Completion

The testimony that God has given you is unique and extraordinary. You have made it through great times of trial and tribulations, so you can now embrace the moments of triumph in your life. Remember how you made it through – by the power of God.

Now, you are preparing to move forward and embrace a greater level of anointing and purpose in your life. Remember how you will make it through – by the power of God.

You have limited power, skills, abilities and vision scope. You cannot make things happen on your own. But when you partner with the Holy Spirit, you can do all things through Christ who strengthens you. It is an awesome opportunity in your life to see a manifestation of God's glory revealed in your story.

It's amazing – you have made it through so much to get to this moment in time. Do not ever take credit for your exaltation in life; **ALL** dominion, honor and majesty belong to the Lord. Seek His power to operate in ways beyond your control. God's plan for your life must be realized through His power.

God's plan for your life must be realized through His power.

Throughout the Bible, there are numerous stories about the people of God receiving salvation, deliverance, wholeness, anointing, strength, and freedom because the power of God was revealed in their situation. Similarly, all that you need can be attained by accessing the power of God. It will bring you through and place you in a precarious place where you must rely upon God every step of the way.

One of my favorite biblical stories is about Joseph in Genesis. Joseph was placed in a pit, forced into slavery, falsely accused and subjected to adverse conditions. Yet, regardless of where he was in the physical realm, he was always in the right place in the spiritual realm. The Bible records that the Lord was always with him and God blessed those around him because of his presence. Ultimately, Joseph made it from the prison to serving as one of the rulers in the nation because of God's power in his life.

Similarly, you have been through moments that would have crushed others, but they have served as places of remembrance in your life and

———†——— plackets to show the progress to your destiny. The Lord is with you. Regardless of what you

You are an overcomer and a conqueror.

face, you are an overcomer and a conqueror.

You cannot fail in the future. You will be a

——————————— great success because it is not your plan; rather, it is the Lord's will concerning your life. The Lord is in chief control and you are simply God's vessel for the promise. Be still, listen for the guidance of the Holy Spirit and follow God's ways in all that you do. You will experience greater in your life that will be recorded on Earth and in Heaven. Many will receive blessings because of your obedience and unselfish leap of faith at this juncture of your life.

Today, focus your prayer and meditation time on the awesome power of God that will propel you to a place of divine promise and position. Greater is coming!

What an amazing accomplishment! You have made it through 21 days and have upgraded your life. You will never be the same again.

I celebrate you. Others will applaud you. Most of all, God empowers you. Your best is yet to come!

Log onto www.delishiadavis.com and download your course completion certificate. You are an overcomer!

Congratulations!

UPGRADE PRAYER

Holy God,

As I come to the close of these 21 days of fasting and prayer, I am filled with gratitude for the journey I have shared with you. I thank you for the strength and endurance you have granted me, and for the moments of intimacy and revelation I have experienced in your presence.

Lord, I lift up my heart to you and ask for your continued favor to rest upon me. May your grace and mercy surround me like a shield as I step boldly into the days ahead. May your divine favor open doors of opportunity and usher me into new levels of blessing and abundance.

Grant me, O Lord, a spirit of excellence in all that I do. May my actions and words reflect the beauty and holiness of your character. Guide my steps and order my path according to your perfect will, that I may walk in the fullness of your purpose for my life.

As I conclude this time of fasting and prayer, may the seeds I have planted in faith bear fruit in due season. Strengthen my resolve to continue seeking you with all my heart, knowing that you are a rewarder of those who diligently seek you.

I commit myself afresh to you, O Lord, surrendering my desires, plans, and dreams into your loving hands. May your kingdom come and your will be done in my life, now and forevermore.

In the mighty name of Jesus, I pray. Amen.

Personal Journey Post Test

Rate your progress
1-Strongly Agree   2– Agree   3–Not Applicable 4_Disagree
5–Strongly Disagree

	1	2	3	4	5
I feel stronger in my spiritual walk.					
I am ready to move forward in life.					
I have made visionary plans for the future.					
I have better relationships with my family and friends.					
My quality of life has improved.					
I have forgiven some people who have wronged me.					
I am a better person as a result of this journey.					
My patience has improved.					
I live in a state of peace with God and others.					
I pray daily.					
Meditation is a part of my daily life.					
I am grateful for the blessings in my life.					
I complain fewer than five times a day.					

My life will never be the same.					
I accepted the Lord Jesus Christ as my Savior.					
I am a better person than I was before this experience.					
Praise is a part of my daily experiences.					
I worship God personally on a regular basis.					
I asked God for forgiveness.					
Others notice a difference in me.					
I am a beneficiary of grace.					
I have experienced great progress in the last 21 days.					
I take time to journal about my development.					
I am saved.					
I am living according to God's will for my life.					

Personal Transformation Success Story

When I began this 21-day journey, I felt…

_____

_____

_____

_____

I learned many things about myself, including…

_____

_____

_____

_____

Today, I have been strengthened by…

_____

_____

_____

_____

I have made decisions to change my life by….

_____

_____

_____

_____

I declare the following over my life…

_____

_____

_____

_____

My dreams and goals are...

_____

_____

_____

_____

I commit to do the following...

_____

_____

_____

_____

I am grateful for....

_____

_____

_____

_____

Success Stories

I am thrilled to endorse DeLishia Davis, a remarkable author, phenomenal preacher, and national leader. DeLishia's profound insights and captivating storytelling ability shine through her work, inspiring readers to embrace personal transformation and spiritual growth. As a preacher, her dynamic presence and powerful messages leave a lasting impact, igniting hearts and minds with hope and empowerment. Pastor Davis' leadership extends far beyond the pulpit, as she fearlessly champions justice and equality on a national scale. Her authenticity, compassion, and unwavering commitment to uplifting others make her a true beacon of light in today's world. I wholeheartedly recommend her work to all seeking inspiration and enlightenment.

Dr. Joseph E. Lowery
Author, Singing the Lord's Song in a Strange Land

I am honored to endorse DeLishia Davis, whose unwavering dedication to social justice shines brightly through her leadership on the board of People for the American Way. DeLishia's passion for equity and fairness is palpable in every word she speaks and every action she takes. Her commitment to advocating for marginalized communities is truly commendable, and her tireless efforts have made a significant impact on the advancement of civil rights and equality. DeLishia's leadership is not just inspiring; it is transformative. I wholeheartedly support her work and encourage others to join her in the fight for a more just and inclusive society.

Norman Lear
Founder, People for the American Way

The devotional materials were an awesome help in keeping me on track throughout each day to focus on my time spent with the Lord, the Word and on my personal transformation. The anointing on Rev. Delishia is so awesome and is shown in every aspect of this 21-day journey. She is a very gifted servant of God!!!

— Rev. Frances Sparkman

While I was on the journey, one of my goals was to launch my website by my birthday. Well, I hadn't worked on my site since October 2014. The Lord had me busy at it on Sunday, January 25, 2015. I just launched my site …Monday, February 26, 2015. A day ahead of schedule. Everything we discussed on the journey made this possible. GOD BLESS YOU ALL!! KEEP IT IN YOUR PRAYERS.

Cassandra Tobias

Now I know him in a better way, at the end of 2014, I was blessed to witness the Lord heal my sister from heart value replacement surgery., She fully recovered in less time than normal and the medical staff was astonished at how well she healed. In times past, I witnessed the Lord heal my mother, so I know his healing power, but I never thought I would get to know him this way, a better way, during the 21-days of transformation I have had confirmation from the Lord about my assignment. He has helped me to understand the dreams that must come to past and now I know that the plans he has for me is not for me alone but to further his kingdom for generations to come. He has taught me that the race is not given to the swift but to the one who endures, and he has helped me to endure.

I see now that we must never stop praying and speaking the Word of God, and trust him, as it is written we must live by every word that proceeds from the mouth of our God. He is always with us as he promised, Our God is an awesome God and he's with us all the time. We must acknowledge his daily presence which I have been guilty of neglecting. I have taken for granted his grace and mercies that are new every day and I ask him to forgive me for that, for he does not deserve that, not after he has sustained me through difficulties, heartache and pains, not after he has comforted and delivered me from those who meant to harm me. I've come to realize that I must honor him and worship him for who he is in my life for I know I belong to him.

This journey has helped to renew my daily devotional time with Jesus. My day feels out of place when I don't start with prayer and studying his word, simply making time for Jesus before staring my day and meditating on his word and believing and trusting in him to bring me thru no matter what the situation maybe, for he has the answer. One thing I have learned is that no one knows how your day will begin or end but the Lord. I plan to continue in this transformation for I believe that the Lord has greatness for all who trust in him.

As I have always said, "To God Be the Glory for the things he has done, for he is alone is worthy."

Thank You so much, Pastor, for your hard work and dedication.

Sis. Doris Covington
Yours in Christ Jesus our Lord.

These 21 Days has changed my life forever! Thank you for sharing this information with me and blessing me.

– Sally Martinez

I can't describe how much better I feel in my body and spirit. This was just what I needed!!! Thank you, Pastor DeLishia Davis. You are an awesome woman of God. I am glad you kept preaching, even after your illness. God kept you here for a reason and thousands have been blessed by this journey. I believe MILLIONS will be blessed with the book release!

– Dr. Michael Little

I am sure this world can identify many people who give because they have the means and opportunity. Those who have committees and point people. But identifying those who give of themselves, their whole self, despite their needs, despite their circumstances, despite their struggle, that is different. That is harder. That is courageous, admirable, unconditional, that is commendable... And it is Pastor DeLishia Davis... selfless in the face of all things, remembering her gift in all moments.

— Kimberley P. Alexander
Registered Nurse–Houston, TX

Pastor Delishia Davis is a true woman of God who is determined to be dedicated to God. Not in just what she says, but also in what she does. In spite of so many obstacles that have formed against her, to discourage her, she still stands firm on the word of God and allows "no weapon formed against" her to "prosper." She IS more than a conqueror through Jesus Christ and I am SO grateful to be able to call her, not just my s0ister, but also my friend.

— Min. Leslie Rice

When I received an invitation to embark upon the "21 Days to Personal Transformation" journey, I knew it came as a Divine response to the deep prayer of my heart to recalibrate my personal walk with the Lord for 2015. Pastor DeLishia Davis is a beloved daughter of the Holy One whose passion for following Christ is manifest so beautifully through these devotions. You will be inspired by her attention to draw forth heart-challenging and life-changing insights from scripture. And if you commit to delving into all three components of the journey – daily devotion, a fast of your choice by the Spirit's leading, and commitment to a circle of accountability and prayer – you will be transformed as you experience prophetic encouragement and prayers and know that indeed "Greater IS Coming!"

— Rev. Ann Jefferson – Director of Community Life & Spiritual Care, Pacific School of Religion – Berkeley, California

"Transformative!" I know, some may be expecting a more creative expression to describe that which has already been pronounced in this title! But Pastor DeLishia Davis has exemplified & provided faithful stewardship in continuing the rich legacy of practicing, disciplining & living a more intimate, closer walk with our GOD, our Savior, & our Lord, in the Master's hand! In the nitty-gritty of the vicissitudes & changing seasons of life, "Break Through to A New You: 21 Days of Personal Transformation" provides a simultaneous practical & loving spiritual model for warmly & effectively integrating a life-changing, closer walk with our Heavenly Father into our daily walk! Take hold of your "Break Through" today! Thank you, Pastor Dee!

— Rev. Stanley R. Wright

"A 'preacher's preacher' from a generational line of distinguished preachers. Sincere about and deeply dedicated to the 'work of the ministry.' A mind to be reckoned with, a voice to be heard."

Khaleifa Lumumba
(Formerly G.R. Patterson) Marywood, California

One of the fascinating roles of the spiritual leader for this twenty-first century is to be able to make relevant the tradition of the church and the reception of such by a technology driven, social media inceptive generation. The days in which we now traverse are filled with doubt of the historical Biblical narrative, the challenge continues of creation v evolution, and the realities of time and opportunity to fully engage one in what is becoming non-traditional acceptance.

It, then, is the spiritual leader who has to be cognitive of the culture, heritage, and stereotypes that exists within the experience of one seeking to make some sense of what is reality and what becomes acceptable amongst the congregation that leader attempts to address and maybe persuade. To further complicate matters is the notion that emotionalism is more important than intellectual in acceptance to the material presented. The leader must be able to present his/her position from a platform that is not only cognitive, but also relative.

And so I am extremely proud of one such leader as Rev. Dee who has the capacity to look beyond the boundaries of traditional approach to also include the relevancy of today's perception of how one's spiritual content and context should be approached. Spurgeon once said that "where there is fire, there must also be light." She is, I feel, uniquely gifted is transforming the "old school" into acceptable mores where the social media and technology has its relevance, but the time honored traditions as not thrown out and discarded like rubbish. She has the gift to exegete the situation and bring forth such opportunity for understanding that makes the intellectual seek out further information while at the same time the emotional will respond as having experienced and learned from the analysis.

Rev. Dee is not by any means bound and gagged by traditional and yet, very steeped in it. She is very cognitive of the present generation, its perception and acceptance, and not caught up in the desire to change simply for the sake of change. She is very studious and open to the ideology of the present age and willing to engage conversation and debate for the future. But she is also engaging of all that she may be better informed and thus in a better posture to develop generational acceptance of the spiritual dynamics that confront our society.

I am honored to know and be personally engaged with such a student and leader as Rev Dee. She brings to me and many others the desire to serve with greater enthusiasm, capture with greater involvement the head as well as the heart, and bring about effective change as necessary.

Rev. Ronald A. Boykin
Pastor, Seaton Memorial A.M.E. Church
Lanham, Maryland

I embarked upon this journey (*21 Days of Personal Transformation*) believing God would do something spectacular in my life and that it would do the same for others who would be led to participate. I tell you the truth — I am forever changed because of this experience and thoughts that remain with me as perpetual blessings to my soul.

I remain in awe of the commitment, preparation, and prayer presented by Pastor Boykin and the select group of pastors, prophets, evangelist, and ministers who without hesitation gave of their hearts, minds, and souls to ensure each session was richly blessed with an on-time word from God.

Each day, we were presented with prayer-focused devotions which served as a catalyst into the very presence of God. Each evening, we were further strengthened and encouraged by the blessed testimonies and reflections of God's greatness in the lives of those who dared to trust the word.

I am blessed each moment as I reflect on the precision and eloquence in which my sister poured out her love for God and for His people. I pray God's continued blessings upon Pastor D. Davis, her family, and all those who will glean from this and future works as she is propelled deeper into her destiny.

Pastor Davis, I return the same prophesy to you that you have so graciously prophesied into the lives of God's people, "Greater is coming!"

With love and admiration,

Lorraine (Pastor B) Burnett-Hill
Soul Matters
Atlanta, Georgia

The 21-Day Transformation devotion from Psalm 51:10 and 11 is a personal admonition to purity. The psalmist says to "Create in me a clean heart O God and renew a right spirit within me." This message followed immediately after the message on "purging (letting go). How timely to allow the cleansing of the Lord, to allow purification by God's power! This calls for an inward journey of dealing with those hidden things of the flesh. Too often we cover up all of the inward struggles, attitudes and impure thoughts that prevent us from walking in the full anointing of the Lord, and we need to be pure. David knew this when he cried out to God for his help.

He also cried out for restoration–"Renew a right spirit within me; cast me not away from your presence, and take not thy holy spirit from me". We must realize that God will not dwell in an unclean temple. We need his cleansing power to get us right so that we can move forward in the purposes and calling of God.

In this personal journey, the intimate time spent in the Lord's presence, with his Word and the assurance of our faith, we can realize how precious it is to be transformed by the purity of a clean heart and by restoration of his Holy Spirit.

Rev. Robin Canty Rolle

Dr. DeLishia Davis has often displayed her prolific gifts as a vibrant orator and a brilliant author, essayist and journalist, but she has established herself as a distinct practical theologian with this work. The superfluities of pointless trendy or hip targeted catch phrases or meaningless anecdotes are completely absent from her writing. I find that she expresses herself with unrestrained lucid imagery and heartfelt sensitivity to all readers. These traits are translated into her superlative writing and are readily identified on each day. I find her ability to appeal to readers at all spiritual levels, whether they are the spiritual novice or the transcendent guru to be absolutely captivating. The spiritual journey that we are invited to embark upon is, indeed, transformative;

however, I find that the journey does not end with the last word on the last page.

Whether the book is used as guided curriculum for a small group or if an individual uses it to help with the broadening of an awareness of self, the results will lead to dramatic transformation and incredible spiritual formation. After one offers careful analysis to the book, there is an intrinsic call to continue the excursion that this book leads us to freely participate in and the reader feels compelled to allocate to others all of the learnings that are gleaned from the magnificent lessons that we learn about ourselves through the challenges that are experienced each day. We are wonderfully stretched beyond our spiritual comfort zones as we are forced to grapple with the words that are highlighted each day. Her unique ability to center the reader on each carefully chosen word causes the conditions to be conducive for spiritual fertility that indeed leads to a bountiful spiritual harvest for each day of the journey.

Rev. Jacson L. Moody
Miles Memorial CME Church
Rockford, Illinois

About the Author

Delishia Davis is a multifaceted force for change, blending her academic achievements with a profound commitment to community service. Graduating from New York University with a degree in Education and graduate certificate in English Literature, she embarked on a journey that seamlessly intertwined her passion for education with her unwavering dedication to social justice.

For 27 years, DeLishia has served as a Methodist Pastor, guiding congregations with empathy and wisdom. As the founder of the New Beginnings Foundation, she has spearheaded initiatives to uplift marginalized communities and foster hope where it's needed most. DeLishia has lived in the United States and abroad, aiding those in need and building relationships to empower others.

In addition to her pastoral duties, DeLishia serves as the Chaplain of the National Council of Negro Women in Northern Virginia, providing spiritual guidance and support to empower women of color. Her leadership extends to the National Association for the Advancement of Colored People, where she holds the esteemed position of Religious Affairs Chairperson of the Arlington branch, advocating for equality and justice on local and national scales.

As a board member for People for the American Way, DeLishia channels her passion for democracy and civil liberties into tangible action, working to protect and expand the rights of all citizens.

Beyond her advocacy work, DeLishia is also a dedicated English Literature teacher, inspiring students with her love for literature and guiding them toward critical thinking and self-discovery.

As a certified professional life coach, DeLishia empowers individuals to overcome obstacles and unlock their full potential. Her coaching philosophy is rooted in empathy, resilience, and a deep belief in the inherent worth of every person.

DeLishia A. Davis has been honored with many distinguished awards to include the Sojourners Award for international missions, Henry L. Holmes Meritorious Award, Pastor of the Year, Rosa Parks Community Service Award, and the NAACP President's Award.

Pastor Davis has served congregations in Ohio, Mississippi, Pennsylvania, New Jersey and Virginia. She is currently the pastor of Calloway United Methodist Church in Arlington, Virginia and leads a fresh expressions ministry in the area.

While her professional accomplishments are vast and impactful, DeLishia's most cherished roles are those of mother to Maya Alexis Davis and Mycah Alexandrea Davis.

Born in Washington, DC, she embodies and instills the values of compassion, justice, and service.

DeLishia Davis' life is a testament to the power of service and the transformative impact of compassion. Through her tireless dedication, she continues to inspire positive change and uplift those in need, leaving an indelible mark on her community and beyond.

www.DeLishiaDavis.com

admin@delishiadavis.com

Printed in the USA
CPSIA information can be obtained
at www.ICGtesting.com
JSHW022037020724
65728JS00001B/4